Microsoft® Office Word 2010: Level 3

About This Course

In *Microsoft® Office Word 2010: Level 2*, you gained all the skills needed to create and format typical business documents. Now, you may need to work on lengthy and more complex documents. In this course, you will use Word to create, manage, revise, and distribute long documents and forms.

Microsoft® Office Word 2010 is much more than a word processing program. It can be used to save documents in a variety of other file formats, to collaborate on complicated business documents, and to manage how documents are accessed and distributed. Gaining an in-depth understanding on the advanced features of Word will enable you to secure, collaborate, and manage long and complex documents effectively.

This course can also benefit you if you are preparing to take the Microsoft Office Specialist (MOS) Certification exams for Microsoft® Word 2010. Please refer to the CD-ROM that came with this course for documents that map exam objectives to the content in the Microsoft Office Word courseware series. To access the mapping documents, insert the CD-ROM into your CD-ROM drive and at the root of the CD, double-click ExamMappingCore.doc or ExamMappingExpert.doc to open a mapping document. In addition to the mapping documents, two assessment files per course can be found on the CD-ROM to check your knowledge. To access the assessments, at the root of the course part number folder, double-click 084584s3.doc to view the assessments without the answers marked, or double-click 084584ie.doc to view the assessments with the answers marked.

If your course manual did not come with a CD-ROM, please go to **http://www.elementk.com/courseware-file-downloads** to download the files.

Course Description

Target Student

This course is designed for persons who want to gain skills necessary to manage lengthy documents, collaborate with others, and secure documents.

Course Prerequisites

Students should be able to use Microsoft® Office Word 2010 to create, edit, format, save, and print business documents that contain text, tables, and graphics. Students should also be able to use a web browser and an email program. In order to understand how Word interacts with other applications in the Microsoft Office System, students should have a basic understanding of how worksheets and presentations work. To ensure your success, you need to first take the following Element K courses or have equivalent knowledge:

- *Microsoft® Office Word 2010: Level 1*
- *Microsoft® Office Word 2010: Level 2*

Course Objectives

In this course, you will create, manage, revise, and distribute documents.

You will:

- Use Word with other programs.
- Collaborate on documents.
- Manage document versions.
- Add reference marks and notes.
- Simplify the use of long documents.
- Secure a document.
- Create forms.

Certification

This course is designed to help you prepare for the following certification.

Certification Path: MOS: Microsoft Office Word 2010 Exam 77–881

Certification Path: MOS: Microsoft Office Word Expert 2010 Exam 77–887

This course is one of a series of Element K courseware titles that addresses Microsoft Office Specialist (MOS) certification skill sets. The MOS and certification program is for individuals who use Microsoft's business desktop software and who seek recognition for their expertise with specific Microsoft products.

How to Use This Book

As a Learning Guide

This book is divided into lessons and topics, covering a subject or a set of related subjects. In most cases, lessons are arranged in order of increasing proficiency.

The results-oriented topics include relevant and supporting information you need to master the content. Each topic has various types of activities designed to enable you to practice the guidelines and procedures as well as to solidify your understanding of the informational material presented in the course.

At the back of the book, you will find a glossary of the definitions of the terms and concepts used throughout the course. You will also find an index to assist in locating information within the instructional components of the book.

In the Classroom

This book is intended to enhance and support the in-class experience. Procedures and guidelines are presented in a concise fashion along with activities and discussions. Information is provided for reference and reflection in such a way as to facilitate understanding and practice.

Each lesson may also include a Lesson Lab or various types of simulated activities. You will find the files for the simulated activities along with the other course files on the enclosed CD-ROM. If your course manual did not come with a CD-ROM, please go to **http:// elementkcourseware.com** to download the files. If included, these interactive activities enable you to practice your skills in an immersive business environment, or to use hardware and software resources not available in the classroom. The course files that are available on the CD-ROM or by download may also contain sample files, support files, and additional reference materials for use both during and after the course.

As a Teaching Guide

Effective presentation of the information and skills contained in this book requires adequate preparation. As such, as an instructor, you should familiarize yourself with the content of the entire course, including its organization and approaches. You should review each of the student activities and exercises so you can facilitate them in the classroom.

Throughout the book, you may see Instructor Notes that provide suggestions, answers to problems, and supplemental information for you, the instructor. You may also see references to "Additional Instructor Notes" that contain expanded instructional information; these notes appear in a separate section at the back of the book. PowerPoint slides may be provided on the included course files, which are available on the enclosed CD-ROM or by download from **http://elementkcourseware.com**. The slides are also referred to in the text. If you plan to use the slides, it is recommended to display them during the corresponding content as indicated in the instructor notes in the margin.

The course files may also include assessments for the course, which can be administered diagnostically before the class, or as a review after the course is completed. These exam-type questions can be used to gauge the students' understanding and assimilation of course content.

As a Review Tool

Any method of instruction is only as effective as the time and effort you, the student, are willing to invest in it. In addition, some of the information that you learn in class may not be important to you immediately, but it may become important later. For this reason, we encourage you to spend some time reviewing the content of the course after your time in the classroom.

As a Reference

The organization and layout of this book make it an easy-to-use resource for future reference. Taking advantage of the glossary, index, and table of contents, you can use this book as a first source of definitions, background information, and summaries.

Course Icons

Icon	Description
	A **Caution Note** makes students aware of potential negative consequences of an action, setting, or decision that are not easily known.
	Display Slide provides a prompt to the instructor to display a specific slide. Display Slides are included in the Instructor Guide only.
	An **Instructor Note** is a comment to the instructor regarding delivery, classroom strategy, classroom tools, exceptions, and other special considerations. Instructor Notes are included in the Instructor Guide only.
	Notes Page indicates a page that has been left intentionally blank for students to write on.
	A **Student Note** provides additional information, guidance, or hints about a topic or task.
	A **Version Note** indicates information necessary for a specific version of software.

Course Requirements

Hardware

For this course, you will need one computer for each student and the instructor. Each computer should have the following hardware configuration:

- A 1 GHz Pentium-class processor or faster.
- A minimum of 256 MB of RAM. (512 MB of RAM is recommended.)
- A 10 GB hard disk or larger. You should have at least 1 GB of free hard disk space available for Office installation.
- A CD-ROM drive.
- A keyboard and mouse or other pointing device.
- A 1024 x 768 resolution monitor is recommended.
- Network cards and cabling for local network access.
- Internet access (contact your local network administrator).
- A printer (optional) or an installed printer driver.
- A projection system to display the instructor's computer screen.

Software

- Microsoft® Office Professional Edition 2010.
- Microsoft® Office Suite Service Pack 1.
- Microsoft® Windows® XP Professional with Service Pack 2.

   This course was developed using the Windows XP operating system; however, the manufacturer's documentation states that it will also run on Vista. If you use Vista, you might notice some slight differences when keying the course.

- Windows Rights Management Services (RMS) Client.

Class Setup

Initial Class Setup

1. Install Windows XP Professional on an empty partition.

   - Leave the Administrator password blank.

   - For all other installation parameters, use values that are appropriate for your environment (see your local network administrator for details).

2. On Windows XP Professional, disable the Welcome screen. (This step ensures that students will be able to log on as the Administrator user regardless of what other user accounts exist on the computer.)

   a. Click **Start** and choose **Control Panel→User Accounts.**

   b. Click **Change The Way Users Log On And Off.**

   c. Uncheck **Use Welcome Screen.**

   d. Click **Apply Options.**

3. For Windows XP Professional, install Service Pack 2. Use the Service Pack installation defaults.

4. On the computer, install a printer driver (a physical print device is optional). Click **Start** and choose **Printers And Faxes.** Under **Printer Tasks,** click **Add A Printer** and follow the prompts.

   If you do not have a physical printer installed, right-click the printer and choose **Pause Printing** to prevent any print error messages.

5. Run the **Internet Connection Wizard** to set up the Internet connection appropriately for your environment, if you did not do so during installation.

6. Display known file type extensions.

   a. Open Windows Explorer (right-click **Start** and then choose **Explore**).

   b. Choose **Tools→Folder Options.**

   c. On the **View** tab, in the **Advanced Settings** list box, uncheck **Hide Extensions For Known File Types.**

   d. Click **Apply,** and then click **OK.**

   e. Close Windows Explorer.

7. Log on to the computer as the Administrator user if you have not already done so.

8. Perform a complete installation of Microsoft Office Professional 2010.

9. Install Microsoft Office Suite Service Pack 1.

10. In the **User Name** dialog box, click **OK** to accept the default user name and initials.

11. In the **Microsoft Office 2010 Activation Wizard** dialog box, click **Next** to activate the Office 2010 application.

12. When the activation of Microsoft Office 2010 is complete, click **Close** to close the **Microsoft Office 2010 Activation Wizard** dialog box.

13. In the **User Name** dialog box, click **OK.**

14. In the **Welcome To Microsoft 2010** dialog box, click **Finish.** You must have an active Internet connection in order to complete this step. Select the **Download And Install Updates From Microsoft Update When Available (Recommended)** option so that whenever there is a new update it gets automatically installed in your system.

15. After the Microsoft Update is run, in the **Microsoft Office** dialog box, click **OK.**

16. Minimize the Language Bar, if necessary.

17. On the course CD-ROM, open the 084584 folder. Then, open the Data folder. Run the 084584dd.exe self-extracting file located in it. This will install a folder named 084584Data on your C drive. This folder contains all the data files that you will use to complete this course. If your course did not come with a CD, please go to **http:// elementkcourseware.com** to download the data files.

Within each lesson folder, you may find a Solution folder. This folder contains solution files for the lesson's activities and lesson lab, which can be used by students to check their end results.

For activities that require complex class setup requirements, simulations are provided. Within each lesson folder, you may find a Simulations folder. If you choose to, you can run the simulations provided to perform the activities in class or to review after class.

Install Windows Rights Management Services (RMS)

To install Windows Rights Management Services (RMS):

1. Launch the Microsoft Office Word 2010 application.

2. Select the **File** tab, and in the Backstage view, in the **Permissions** section, from the **Protect Document** drop-down list, select **Restrict Permission by People→Manage Credentials.**

3. In the **Microsoft Office** message box, click **Yes.**

4. In the **File Download - Security Warning** message box, click **Run.**

5. In the **Internet Explorer - Security Warning** message box, click **Run** to execute the file.

6. In the **Windows Rights Management Client with Service Pack 2** dialog box, on the **Welcome to the Windows Rights Management Client with Service Pack 2 Setup Wizard** page, click **Next.**

7. On the **License Agreement** page, select the **I Agree** option and click **Next.**

8. On the **Confirm Installation** page, click **Next.**

9. On the **Installation Complete** page, click **Close.**

10. In the Backstage view, from the **Protect Document** drop-down list, select**Restrict Permission by People→Manage Credentials.**

11. In the **Service Sign-Up** dialog box, select **Yes, I want to sign up for this free service from Microsoft** and click **Next.**

12. In the **Security Alert** message box, click **OK.**

13. In the **Windows Rights Management** wizard, on the **Welcome to the Information Rights Management Configuration Wizard** page, select **Yes, I have a Windows Live ID** and click **Next.**

14. In the **Sign in to Windows Live** page, in the **Sign in to IRM** section, in the **Email address** text box, enter your Hotmail or Windows Live ID, and in the **Password** text box, type the password. Select **Always ask for my email address and password** and then click **Sign in.**

15. On the **Select computer type** page, verify that **This is a private computer** is selected and click **I accept.**

16. On the **Completing the Information Rights Management Configuration Wizard** page, click **Finish.**

Customize the Windows Desktop

Customize the Windows desktop to display the **My Computer** and **My Network Place**s icons on the student and instructor systems:

1. Right-click the desktop and choose **Properties.**

2. Select the **Desktop** tab.

3. Click **Customize Desktop.**

4. In the **Desktop Items** dialog box, check **My Computer** and **My Network Places.**

5. Click **OK** and click **Apply.**

6. Close the **Display Properties** dialog box.

Before Every Class

1. Log on to the computer as the Administrator user.

2. Delete the existing C:\084584Data folder and extract a fresh copy of the course data files from the CD-ROM provided with the course manual or download the data files from **http://elementkcourseware.com.**

1 | Using Microsoft Office Word 2010 with Other Programs

Lesson Time: 30 minutes

Lesson Objectives:

In this lesson, you will use Word with other programs.

You will:

- Link a Word document to an Excel worksheet.
- Send a document outline to PowerPoint.
- Send a document as an email message.

Introduction

You used Microsoft Word to work with various types of documents. You can add other programs to Word to extend its capabilities beyond the scope of word processing. In this lesson, you will use Word with other Office applications such as Excel and PowerPoint.

Using Word to interact with other applications enables you to share and update data from a variety of sources. Similarly, you can work on data present in Word from different applications. The level of integrity among applications ensures that information is processed in a consistent manner, leaving no room for errors.

TOPIC A

Link a Word Document to an Excel Worksheet

You are familiar with creating and customizing information in a Word document. In the course of your work, you may need to use information from other applications while ensuring that the information stays current. In this topic, you will link to data in an Excel worksheet.

Assume that you need to create a table in Word using data from an Excel worksheet. Rather than retyping data and risking typographical errors, you can create a dynamic link to the Excel worksheet containing the desired data. This way, you will avoid data entry mistakes and ensure that any updates made to the source worksheet are reflected in the Word document.

Data Linking

Data linking is the process of linking a text or graphic object to a data source. When an object is linked to a source, the data remains stored in the source and a replica of the source information is displayed in the object. When the source is updated, the linked object is also automatically updated. Data linking helps maintain consistency between a data source and a linked object while keeping the data up to date.

How to Link a Word Document to an Excel Worksheet

Procedure Reference: Establish a Link Between a Word Document and an Excel Worksheet

To link a Word document with an Excel worksheet:

1. Open a Word document in which you want to create a linked object and an Excel worksheet containing the source data.
2. In the Word document, select a location for the linked object.
3. Switch to the Excel worksheet and select the entire worksheet, or a range of cells, or the object that you want to copy.
4. Copy the selected content.
5. Switch to the Word document. On the **Home** tab, in the **Clipboard** group, click the **Paste** drop-down and choose **Paste Special** to launch the **Paste Special** dialog box.
6. Select the **Paste link** option.
7. In the **As** list box, select **Microsoft Office Excel Worksheet Object.**
8. Click **OK** to insert the selected content and link it to the Excel worksheet.

Procedure Reference: Modify and Update Information in a Linked Worksheet Object

To modify information in a linked worksheet object:

1. Display the data source.
   - Double-click a linked worksheet object.
   - Or, right-click a linked worksheet object and choose **Linked Worksheet Object→ Open Link.**

2. Modify the data in the source file, as desired.

3. Switch to the Word document.

4. Right-click the linked worksheet object and choose **Update Link** to update the linked worksheet object.

Obsolete Links

Over the course of a document's life cycle, you may find that some links are no longer relevant and should be removed from the document. This can be done by breaking obsolete links.

Procedure Reference: Break an Obsolete Link

To break a link:

1. Right-click a linked worksheet object and choose **Linked Worksheet Object→Links** to display the **Links** dialog box.

2. Select the desired linked worksheet object and click **Break Link.**

3. In the **Microsoft Word** warning message box, click **Yes.**

4. Click **OK** to close the **Links** dialog box.

ACTIVITY 1-1
Linking a Word Document to an Excel Worksheet

Data Files:

C:\084584Data\Using Word 2010 with Other Programs\Monthly Numbers Memo.docx,
C:\084584Data\Using Word 2010 with Other Programs\Monthly Sales Data.xlsx

Before You Begin

The Microsoft Word application is open.

Scenario:

You have a memo on sales data that you'd like to share with others. The last time you circulated such a memo, you received feedback that it did not contain enough information. So you have made sure that the memo you now possess has the most current monthly sales numbers for each office.

1. Insert a linked worksheet object.

    a. From the C:\084584Data\Using Word 2010 with Other Programs folder, open the Monthly Numbers Memo.docx and Monthly Sales Data.xlsx files.

    b. In the Word document, scroll down to the end and place the insertion point after the last paragraph.

    c. Switch to the **Monthly Sales Data.xlsx - Microsoft Excel** window and select cells A3 through E6.

    d. Right-click cell E6 and choose **Copy.**

    e. Switch to the **Monthly Numbers Memo.docx - Microsoft Word** window.

    f. On the **Home** tab, in the **Clipboard** group, click the **Paste** drop-down and select **Paste Special** to open the **Paste Special** dialog box.

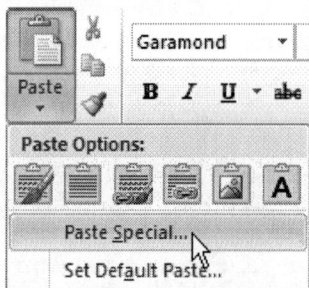

    g. Select the **Paste link** option.

h.   In the **As** list box, select **Microsoft Excel Worksheet Object** and click **OK** to insert the monthly sales numbers as a linked worksheet object.

	North	South	East	Total
January	1.7	3.9	4.7	10.3
February	2.1	3.2	4.4	9.7
March				0.0

2. Update the linked worksheet object with March sales data.

   a.   Double-click the linked worksheet object to display the Monthly Sales Data.xlsx file.

   b.   In cell B6, type **4.1** to include the March data for the North office and press **Tab** to move to the next cell.

   c.   In cells C6 and D6, include the data for the South and East offices as **5.3** and **6.0** respectively and press **Tab.**

   d.   Switch to the **Monthly Numbers Memo.docx - Microsoft Word** window.

3. Update the linked worksheet object.

   a.   Right-click the linked worksheet object and choose **Update Link.**

   b.   Observe that the linked worksheet object is updated with the March data for the North, South, and East offices.

	North	South	East	Total
January	1.7	3.9	4.7	10.3
February	2.1	3.2	4.4	9.7
March	4.1	5.3	6.0	15.4

   c.   Save the Word document as **My Monthly Numbers Memo** and close it.

   d.   Save the Excel worksheet as **My Monthly Sales Data** and close the Excel application.

TOPIC B

Send a Document Outline to Microsoft® Office PowerPoint®

You have linked Word with Excel data. Not only can Word receive information from other programs, but it can also provide information to other programs. In this topic, you will use an existing Word document outline to create a presentation.

You can create a presentation with a blank slide and then go about adding more slides, titles, and text. However, this method is time-consuming and leaves room for errors. A better method would be creating a presentation automatically from a Word document.

Outline View

The purpose of Word's Outline view is to show how a document's contents are organized. You can reorganize the contents in a document using the tools in the **Outline Tools** group. The **Outline Tools** group can be accessed from the **Outlining** tab.

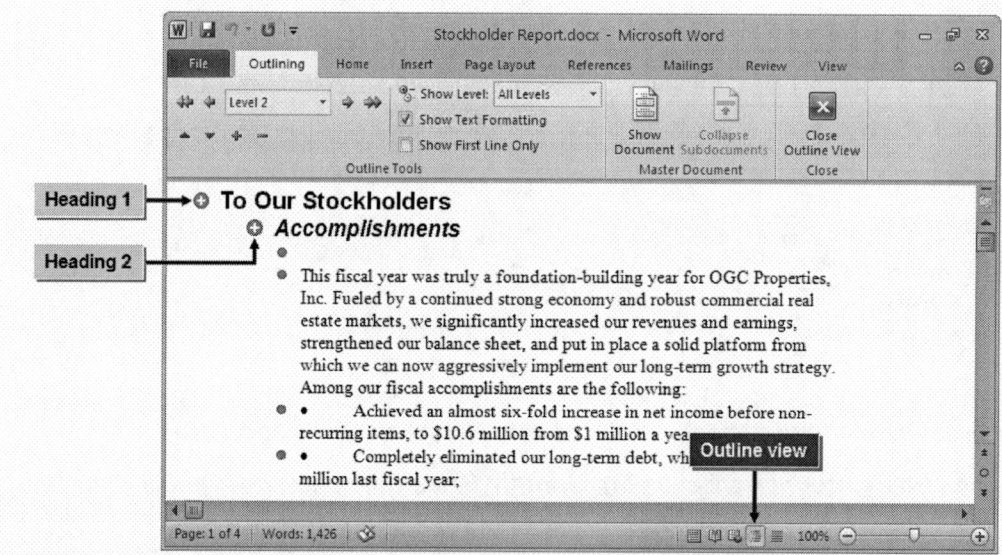

Figure 1-1: The Outline view displays how a document's contents are organized.

Heading Styles and Slides

A document's headings determine where the heading text will be placed in a PowerPoint slide. When a document's outline is sent to PowerPoint, text formatted with the **Heading 1** style becomes a new slide's title. Text formatted with the **Heading 2** style becomes a first-level bullet point. Each subsequent heading level in the document corresponds with a bullet point level in a slide.

Levels

Levels are a way to organize the visibility of contents in a presentation. From the **Show Level** drop-down list, you can select which levels to show in the presentation. The selected level and all higher levels will be visible.

The Outlining Tab

The **Outlining** tab appears when the document is displayed in the **Outline** view. This tab contains groups of options to create, edit, and format the content in a document.

The Outline Tools Group

The **Outline Tools** group contains options that help format the content in a document.

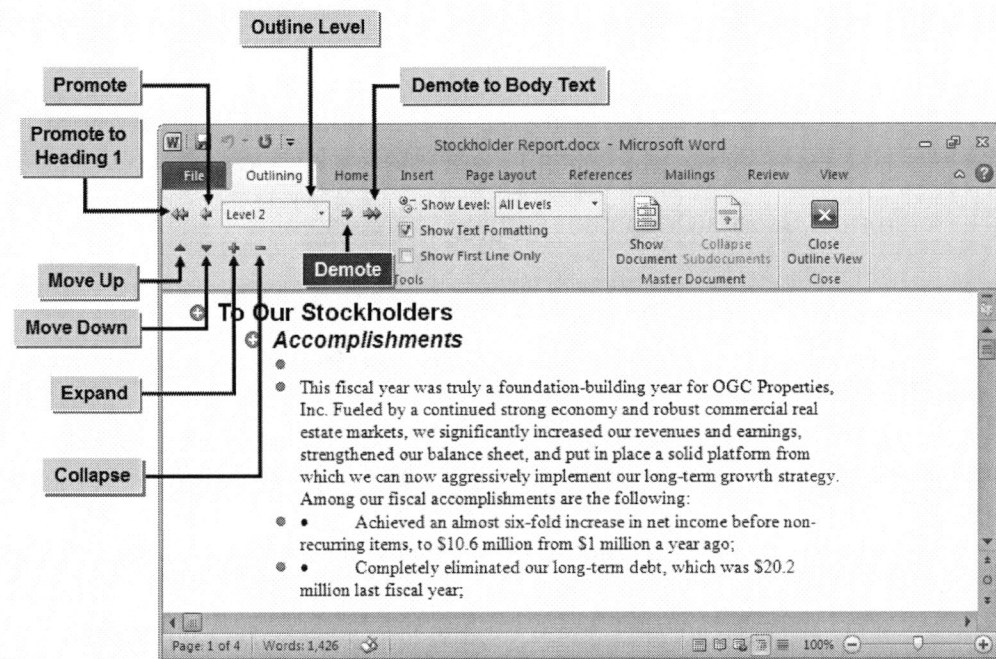

Figure 1-2: *Options in the Outline Tools group that help format the contents in a document.*

Option	Description
Promote to Heading 1	Promotes the selected text to the highest level of the outline.
Promote	Promotes the selected text to a higher level.
Outline Level	Chooses the outline level for the selected text.
Demote	Demotes the selected text to a lower level.
Demote to Body Text	Demotes the selected text to the lowest level of the outline.
Move Up	Moves the selected text up within the outline.
Move Down	Moves the selected text down within the outline.
Expand	Expands the selected text.
Collapse	Collapses the selected text.
Show Level	Choose which level should be displayed in the outline. The selected level and all higher levels will be visible.
Show Text Formatting	Shows or hides text formatting for the outline.
Show First Line Only	Shows or hides only the first line of each paragraph.

How to Send a Document Outline to Microsoft® Office PowerPoint®

Procedure Reference: Add a Command to the Quick Access Toolbar

To add a command to the Quick Access toolbar:

1. On the **File** tab, click **Options.**
2. In the **Word Options** dialog box, select **Quick Access Toolbar.**
3. From the **Choose commands from** drop-down list, select **All Commands.**
4. In the **Choose commands from** list box, scroll down and select the desired command.
5. Click **Add** to add the selected command to the Quick Access toolbar.
6. Click **OK** to close the **Word Options** dialog box and add the command to the Quick Access toolbar.

Procedure Reference: Send a Document Outline to PowerPoint

To send a document outline to PowerPoint:

1. Display a document in the **Outline** view.
   - On the **View** tab, in the **Document Views** group, click **Outline** to display the document in the outline view.
   - Or, on the Microsoft Office status bar, click the **Outline** button to display the document in the **Outline** view and verify whether the headings are displayed at the appropriate levels.
2. If necessary, use the options in the **Outline Tools** group to format the content in the document.
3. If necessary, in the **Close** group, click **Close Outline View** to close the outline view and return to editing the document.
4. On the Quick Access toolbar, click the **Send to Microsoft PowerPoint** button.
5. Press the **Page Down** or **Page Up** key to review the slides and ensure that they appear as intended.
6. If necessary, make modifications to the slides.
7. Save the presentation.

Procedure Reference: Reorganize a Document Outline

To reorganize a document outline:

1. Display a document in the **Outline** view.
2. Reposition content in the outline.
   - Move the mouse pointer over a bullet point, and when it turns into a four-sided arrow, click and drag the bullet point before or after another bullet point to reposition it.
   - Place the insertion point in a bullet point, and on the **Outlining** tab, in the **Outline Tools** group, click the **Move Up** or **Move Down** button to move the content.

3. Change the level of content.

- Move the mouse pointer over a bullet, and when it turns into a four-sided arrow, click and drag the bullet point horizontally to the left or right to promote or demote the content.

- Place the insertion point in a bullet point, and on the **Outlining** tab, in the **Outline Tools** group, click the **Promote** or **Demote** button.

- Place the insertion point in a bullet point, and on the **Outlining** tab, in the **Outline Tools** group, click the **Promote to Heading 1** or **Demote to Body Text** button to promote the point to the highest level or demote it to the lowest level.

4. If necessary, collapse or expand a heading.

- Double-click a bullet with a plus symbol to toggle between expanding or collapsing it.

- Place the insertion point in a bullet point, and on the **Outlining** tab, in the **Outline Tools** group, click the **Expand** or **Collapse** button.

ACTIVITY 1-2
Sending a Document Outline to PowerPoint

Data Files:

C:\084584Data\Using Word 2010 with Other Programs\Stockholder Report.docx

Scenario:

Your manager has asked you to create a PowerPoint presentation based on the latest stockholder report. She needs it quickly, so you need to use the most efficient method for generating the presentation.

---

1. Add the **Send to Microsoft PowerPoint** command to the Quick Access toolbar.

    a. On the **File** tab, click **Options.**

    b. In the **Word Options** dialog box, select **Quick Access Toolbar.**

    c. From the **Choose commands from** drop-down list, select **All Commands.**

    d. In the **Choose commands from** list box, scroll down and select **Send to Microsoft PowerPoint.**

    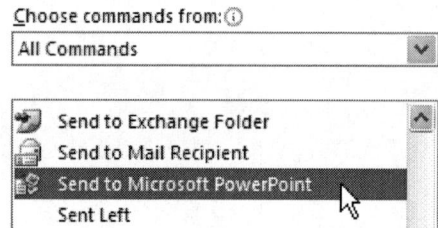

    e. Click **Add** to add the **Send to Microsoft PowerPoint** command to the Quick Access toolbar.

    f. Click **OK** to close the **Word Options** dialog box.

    g. Observe that the **Send to Microsoft PowerPoint** command is added to the Quick Access toolbar.

    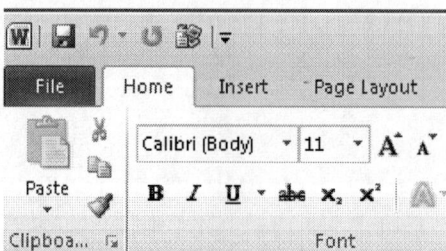

---

2. Display the report in Outline view.

a. From the C:\084584Data\Using Word 2010 with Other Programs folder, open the Stockholder Report.docx file.

b. On the **View** tab, in the **Document Views** group, click **Outline** to switch to the Outline view.

c. On the **Outlining** tab, in the **Outline Tools** group, from the **Show Level** drop-down list, select **Level 3** to show the third outline level in the outline.

- **To Our Stockholders**
  - *Accomplishments*
  - *Mapping to Strategy*
- **Review of Results**
  - *Financial Overview*
    - Net Income
    - Bottom Line
- **Today's Opportunities**
  - *Organizational Restructuring*
    - New Relocation Team

3. Generate the PowerPoint presentation.

a. On the Quick Access toolbar, click the **Send to PowerPoint** button to create a PowerPoint presentation based on the document's outline.

b. Review the slides by pressing **Page Down** four times until the last slide is displayed.

c. Display the **Save As** dialog box.

d. Navigate to the C:\084584Data\Using Word 2010 with Other Programs folder.

e. Save the presentation as *My Stockholder Report* and close the PowerPoint application.

f. Close the **Navigation** pane.

g. Save the Word document as *My Stockholder Report*

h. If necessary, in the **Microsoft Word** message box, click **OK.**

i. Close the Word document.

TOPIC C
Send a Document as an Email Message

You know how to send a document outline to PowerPoint. Once you have the desired content in a document, you may need to send a copy of that document to someone outside of your internal network. In this topic, you will send a document as an email message.

Typically, when you create a document and want to email it to your colleagues for their feedback or review, you would first need to save the document, then open any email client application, attach the document, specify the recipients, and finally send the email. Word simplifies the entire process. You can now turn a document into email message text without exiting the Word application.

The Send Using E-Mail Option

The **Send Using E-Mail** option allows you to send documents to other users. Word has various options for sharing documents.

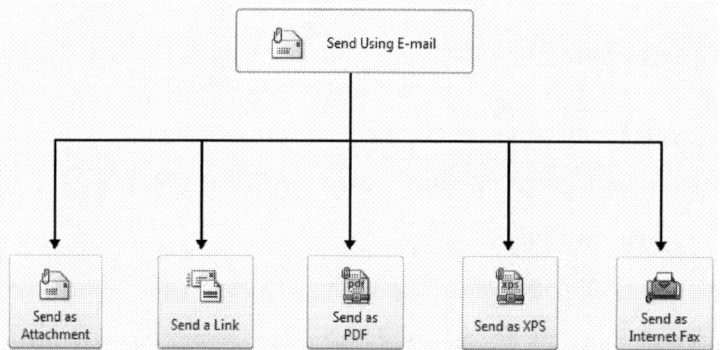

Figure 1-3: Options for sending documents by email.

Option	Allows You To
Send as Attachment	Send a copy of a document as an attachment to the email addresses specified.
Send a Link	Send a link to a shared location in which a document is placed. This option is enabled only when a shared location is created and specified in Word.
Send as PDF	Attach a copy of a document in the PDF format to an email address.
Send as XPS	Attach a copy of a document in the XPS format to an email address.
Send as Internet Fax	Send a document as an Internet fax. For this option to work, you need to be registered with a fax service provider.

How to Send a Document as an Email Message

Procedure Reference: Send a Document as Email Text Using the Send to Mail Recipient Command

To send a document as email text using the **Send to Mail Recipient** command:

1. Open the document you want to send to a mail recipient.

2. If necessary, add the **Send to Mail Recipient** button to the Quick Access toolbar.

3. On the Quick Access toolbar, click the **Send to Mail Recipient** button to open Outlook and email the document as text inside the message.

4. If necessary, make changes to the document.

5. In the **To** text box, type the email address(es) of the primary mail recipient(s).

 Separate multiple recipient addresses with semicolons.

6. If necessary, in the **Cc** text box, type the email address(es) of the recipient(s) you want to copy in on the email.

7. In the **Subject** text box, type the subject of the email.

8. If necessary, in the **Introduction** text box, type an introduction.

9. Click **Send a Copy** to send the document.

Procedure Reference: Send a Document Using the Send Using E-Mail Option

To send a document using the **Send Using E-Mail** option:

1. Open the desired document.

2. On the **File** tab, click **Save and Send.** By default, the **Send Using E-mail** category is selected.

3. Send the document in the desired format via email.

 The **Send a Link** option is available only if you have first saved the document to a web server.

DISCOVERY ACTIVITY 1-3
Sending a Document as an Email Message

Data Files:

C:\084584Data\Using Word 2010 with Other Programs\Simulations\Sending a Document as an Email Message_guided.exe

Setup:

This is a simulated activity that requires Microsoft Exchange Server 2010 and Microsoft® Office Outlook®. In this simulation, your editor is Mary Coleman and her email address is mcoleman@ourglobalcompany.com.

Scenario:

You have to send a story to your editor at mcoleman@ourglobalcompany.com for her review and feedback.

1. To launch the simulation, navigate to the C:\084584Data\Using Word 2010 with Other Programs\Simulations folder.

2. Double-click the **Sending a Document as an Email Message_guided.exe** file.

3. Maximize the simulation window.

4. Follow the onscreen steps for the simulation.

5. When you have finished the activity, close the simulation window.

Lesson 1 Follow-up

In this lesson, you used Word to interact with other programs and extract information from them. Word's ability to interact with other programs helps you to reuse existing content and maintain parity with data sources.

1. **What are the advantages of using Word with Excel?**

2. **In what situations would you prefer to use Word with PowerPoint?**

2 | Collaborating on Documents

Lesson Time: 1 hour(s), 15 minutes

Lesson Objectives:

In this lesson, you will collaborate on documents.

You will:

● Modify user information.

● Send a document for review.

● Review a document.

● Compare document changes.

● Merge documents.

● Review track changes and comments.

● Coauthor documents.

Introduction

You have linked and shared document data. There are times when you will work in a collaborative environment where others will provide feedback and document changes. In this lesson, you will collaborate on documents.

In works that involve collaboration, it is imperative to track all changes made to a project or file by multiple resources. The advanced tracking and coauthoring features in Word come with synchronized capabilities that foster a collaborative work environment.

TOPIC A
Modify User Information

You interacted with other programs using Word 2010. Now you will interact with other users to collaborate on a document. In this topic, you will include user information in Word.

What if you had to take over working on a high-profile company document because the original author was re-assigned? Because this type of company document usually goes through an editing and review process, you would need to modify the user information on the document, so that all the document collaborators clearly identify you as the person who will be making the revisions.

Collaboration Stages

Collaborating on a document usually occurs in stages.

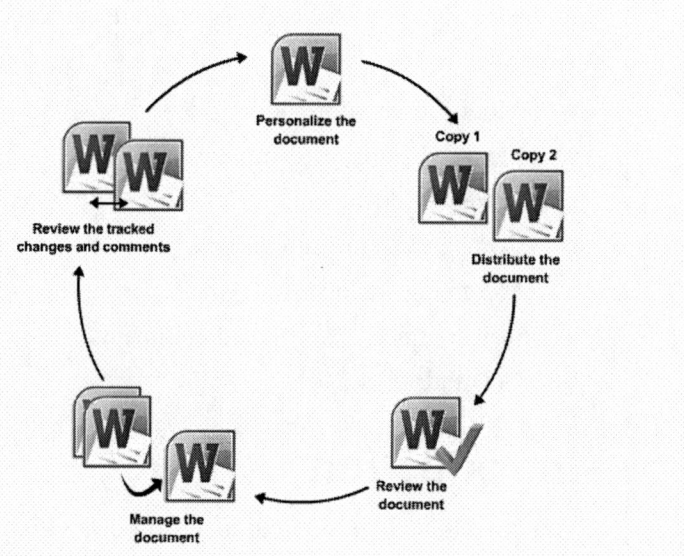

Figure 2-1: *Stages in a collaboration.*

Stage	Requires You To
Personalizing	Include user information that identifies you as the author of a document or a person who has worked on it.
Distributing	Distribute the document to those collaborating with you.
Reviewing	Modify the document as needed by enabling track changes and inserting comments, then return the document.
Managing	Compare and merge the changes into a single document.
Reviewing the tracked changes and comments	Review the changes, accepting and rejecting them as needed. If necessary, begin the collaboration process again.

The Document Properties Panel

The **Document Properties** panel is displayed above the current document. You can display the panel using the **Show Document Panel** option in the **Info** section of the **File** tab. This panel gives you basic details about a document, such as its author, title, subject, and keywords that help in its identification. Though the panel properties can be automatically synchronized with a document's contents, you can customize the panel by adding or removing properties from it.

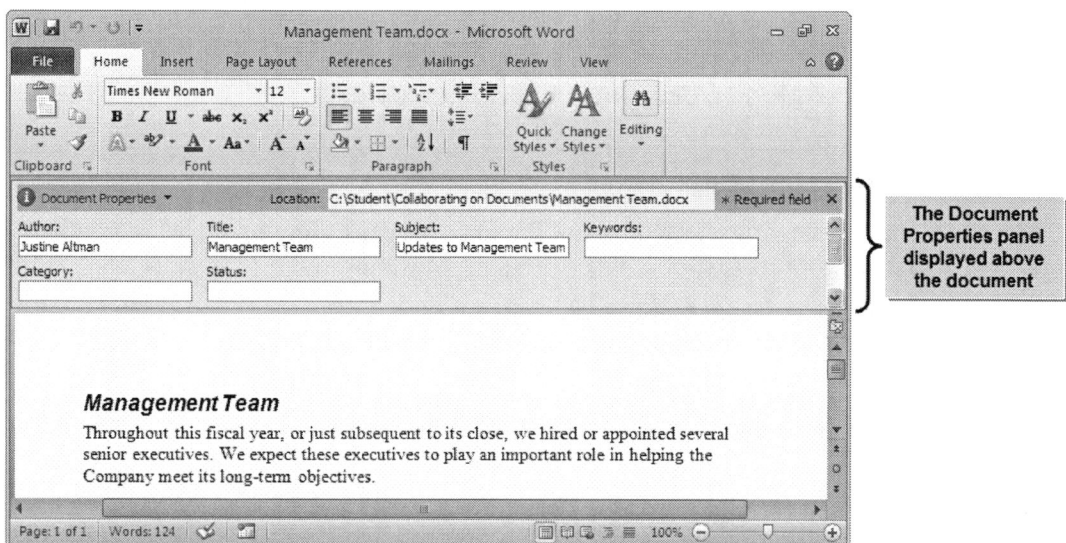

Figure 2-2: The basic details of a document as displayed in the Document Properties panel.

The Properties Dialog Box

You can open the **Properties** dialog box using the **Advanced Properties** option in the **Info** section of the **File** tab. It consists of various tabs, including **General, Summary, Statistics, Contents,** and **Custom.**

Tab	Contains Information On
General	File name and size; type of document; when the file was created, modified, and last accessed; and any file attributes.
Summary	Title, subject, author, manager, company, category, keywords, comments, and the hyperlink base of a document.
Statistics	When the file was created, modified, last accessed, and printed; who last saved the document; the revision number; the total editing time; and word count statistics.
Contents	The document contents.
Custom	Built-in and custom fields you can use to include a wider variety of information about the document.

View the Automatically Updated Properties for a Document

In Word, you can view the properties of a document directly in the backstage view. With the **Info** category selected on the **File** tab, you can view the properties in the right pane of the document.

How to Modify User Information

Procedure Reference: View the Automatically Updated Properties for a Document in the Properties Dialog Box

To view the automatically updated properties for a document:

1. On the **File** tab, in the right pane, from the **Properties** drop-down list, select **Advanced Properties.**

2. In the [document] Properties dialog box, select the desired tab to view the values for each of the properties and click **OK.**

Procedure Reference: Modify User Information

To modify user information:

1. Display the **Word Options** dialog box.

2. With the **General** category selected, in the **Personalize your copy of Microsoft Office** section, in the **User name** text box, type the name you want to use to identify yourself to other collaborators.

3. In the **Initials** text box, type the initials to be displayed and click **OK.**

 The user information that you type in Word will be used in all Office 2010 programs.

Procedure Reference: Update a Document's Properties

To update a document's properties:

1. On the **File** tab, in the right pane, click the **Properties** drop-down, and choose **Advanced Properties.**

2. If necessary, update the summary information.

    a. Select the **Summary** tab.

    b. If necessary, delete the existing information in the desired text boxes.

    c. Type in the summary information in the desired text boxes.

3. If necessary, update the custom information.

    a. Select the **Custom** tab.

    b. In the **Name** list box, select a built-in property name or, in the **Name** text box, type the name for a new custom property.

    c. If necessary, from the **Type** drop-down list, select the desired content type of the custom property.

    d. In the **Value** text box, type the value of the custom property.

 If you select **Yes or no** as the type of the custom property, the **Value** section displays **Yes** and **No** options, with the **Yes** option selected by default.

    e. Click **Add** and click **OK.**

4. Save the document to store the new properties.

ACTIVITY 2-1
Modifying User Information

Data Files:

C:\084584Data\Collaborating on Documents\Management Team.docx

Scenario:

You have been assigned to work on the Management Team document on a temporary basis. Since the document is part of a larger collaborative process, you have been asked to update your user information so that the changes you make to the document are attributable to you.

---

1. Change the user name and initials.

    a. From the C:\084584Data\Collaborating on Documents folder, open the Management Team.docx file.

    b. Select the **File** tab, and in the Backstage view, in the right pane, in the **Related People** section, notice that the **Last Modified By** property is set to Justine Altman who last saved the document.

    c. Display the **Word Options** dialog box.

    d. With the **General** category selected, in the **Personalize your copy of Microsoft Office** section, in the **User name** text box, type your name and press **Tab**.

    e. In the **Initials** text box, type your initials and click **OK**.

---

2. Update the document with the necessary information.

    a. Place the insertion point at the end of the third bullet point, and press **Enter**.

        • Pat Markus, President, Central Region
        • Daniel Ortiz, President, Western Region
        • Chris Johnson, President, Eastern Region
        •

    b. Type *Brian Rodriguez, President, Southern Region*

    c. Under the "Relocation Services" heading, in the first line, double-click the word "three" and type *four*

    d. Save the document as *My Management Team*

    e. Select the **File** tab, to view the document properties.

    f. In the right pane, in the **Related People** section, notice that the **Last Modified By** property is set to the user name you entered.

    g. Close the document.

TOPIC B

Send a Document for Review

You personalized a document by modifying user information. Now you are ready to work on a new project that requires other team members to review your documents. In this topic, you will send a document for review.

Instead of handing out hard copies of the document to the project team, sending it by email is a convenient way to distribute the document. It also helps you to keep track of the document and its reviewers.

How to Send a Document for Review

Procedure Reference: Send a Document as an Attachment

To send a document as an attachment:

1. Open the desired document.
2. Click the **File** tab, select **Save & Send**, and choose **Send Using E-mail**→**Send as Attachment** to display the document's Message window.
3. In the **To** text box, type the email address(es) of the primary mail recipient(s).
4. If necessary, in the **Cc** text box, type the email address(es) of the recipient(s) you want to copy in on the email.
5. In the **Subject** text box, type the subject of the email.
6. If necessary, type a message in the body of the email.
7. Click **Send.**

 Depending on how Outlook is set up, you may need to launch the application and click the **Send/Receive** button to send a document for review.

DISCOVERY ACTIVITY 2-2
Sending a Document as an Attachment

Data Files:

C:\084584Data\Collaborating on Documents\Simulations\Sending a Document as an Attachment_guided.exe

Setup:

This is a simulated activity that requires Microsoft Exchange Server 2010 and Microsoft Office Outlook. In this simulation, your editors are Mary Coleman and Sue Roe, and their email addresses are mcoleman@ourglobalcompany.com and sroe@ourglobalcompany.com, respectively. Your manager is Todd Lite and his email address is tlite@ourglobalcompany.com.

Scenario:

Now that the Management Team document is complete, you need to send it for review. You require feedback for this document by the end of next week, but you aren't sure who will be editing the document. So, you decide to mail the document as an attachment to the two editors in your project team and also copy your manager in on the document.

---

1. To launch the simulation, browse to the C:\084584Data\Collaborating on Documents\ Simulations folder.

---

2. Double-click the **Sending an Email Attachment_guided.exe** file.

---

3. Maximize the simulation window.

---

4. Follow the onscreen steps for the simulation.

---

5. When you have finished the activity, close the simulation window.

TOPIC C
Review a Document

You know how to send documents for review. During a document's review, you may want to keep track of the changes made to the document or explain why some changes were made. In this topic, you will track changes to a document.

When reviewing a hard copy of a document, it is difficult for you to keep track of all the changes. When multiple reviewers work on the same document, it can lead to further confusion. Tracking changes in a Word document eliminates the possibility of missing out suggestions provided by reviewers.

The Track Changes Option

The **Track Changes** option in the **Tracking** group on the **Review** tab allows you to identify the reviewers of a document and their modifications.

Option	Used To
Track Changes	Enable or disable track changes.
Change Tracking Options	Customize the appearance of the editing markup and comments using the **Track Changes Options** dialog box.
Change User Name	Display the **Word Options** dialog box that can be used to change the user information provided.

 With the help of the **Track Changes** indicator, you can identify whether the Track Changes feature is on. You can enable the indicator by right-clicking the status bar and choosing **Track Changes.**

The Track Changes Options Dialog Box

The **Track Changes Options** dialog box allows you to customize the appearance of edited contents in a document. The **Track Changes** options are categorized into various sections.

Section	Used To
Markup	Format insertions, deletions, line alignment, and comments.
Moves	Format and track the different move actions.
Table Cell Highlighting	Apply colors for inserting, deleting, splitting, and merging table cells.
Formatting	Track the formatting changes made to the contents.
Balloons	Specify the formatting changes, insertions, deletions, and comments that need to be displayed in a balloon. It also allows you to specify the width of the balloon, align the balloon, and show or hide the lines connecting the balloon to the text.

The Comments Group

The **Comments** group options enable you to add, delete, and navigate through comments.

Option	Enables you to
New Comment	Insert a new comment in a document.
Delete	Remove comments from a document.
	• **Delete**: Removes a particular comment.
	• **Delete All Comments Shown**: Removes all comments that are visible.
	• **Delete All Comments in Document**: Removes all comments, including those that are hidden.
Previous/Next	Navigate through comments within a document.

How to Review a Document

Procedure Reference: Customize the Track Changes Display

To customize the display of track changes:

1. Open the document in which you want to track changes.
2. On the **Review** tab, in the **Tracking** group, click the **Track Changes** drop-down and choose **Change Tracking Options.**
3. In the **Track Changes Options** dialog box, specify the desired options and click **OK** to customize the display of track changes.

Procedure Reference: Enable Track Changes in a Document

To enable track changes in a document:

1. Set to record track changes.
   * Right-click the Microsoft Office status bar and choose **Track Changes** to enable track changes.
   * Or, enable track changes using the **Review** tab.
      a. On the Ribbon, select the **Review** tab.
      b. On the **Review** tab, in the **Tracking** group, click the **Track Changes** button or click the **Track Changes** drop-down and choose **Track Changes.**
2. If necessary, display the **Word Options** dialog box and update the user information.
3. Review the document and make changes, as necessary.
4. If necessary, disable track changes.
   * On the **Review** tab, in the **Tracking** group, click the **Track Changes** button.
   * Or, in the Microsoft Office status bar, click **Track Changes.**

Procedure Reference: Insert or Delete a Comment

To insert or delete a comment:

1. Select the location for the comment.

    ● Select the text you want to comment on.

    ● Or, place the insertion point where you want to insert a comment.

2. On the **Review** tab, in the **Comments** group, click **New Comment** to insert a comment.

3. Type the comment in the comment balloon.

4. If necessary, place the insertion point in the comment balloon and edit it.

5. If necessary, delete a comment balloon.

    a. Place the insertion point in the comment balloon.

    b. Delete the comment balloon in the document.

       ● On the **Review** tab, in the **Comments** group, click the **Delete** button.

       ● On the **Review** tab, in the **Comments** group, click the **Delete** drop-down arrow and choose the desired option.

       ● Or, right-click a comment and choose **Delete Comment.**

 Position the insertion point over any markup or comment balloon to display the reviewer's name.

ACTIVITY 2-3
Reviewing a Document

Data Files:

C:\084584Data\Collaborating on Documents\Milestones.docx

Scenario:

You have been included in the review cycle of Milestones.docx. Before you enable track changes and begin marking up the document, you decide to modify the track changes options to be consistent with the other reviewers. The options include:

- Insertions Color: Green
- Deletions Color: Red
- Comments: Turquoise
- Balloons: Only used for comments and formatting

---

1. In the **Word Options** dialog box, specify the user name and initials.

    a. From the C:\084584Data\Collaborating on Documents folder, open the Milestones.docx file.

    b. On the **Review** tab, in the **Tracking** group, click the **Track Changes** drop-down and choose **Change User Name.**

    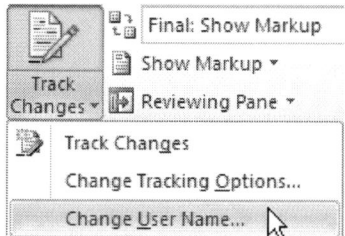

    c. In the **Word Options** dialog box, in the **Personalize your copy of Microsoft Office** section, type your first name, last name, and your initials and click **OK.**

---

2. Modify the options in the **Markup** and **Balloons** sections.

    a. In the **Tracking** group, click the **Track Changes** drop-down and choose **Change Tracking Options.**

    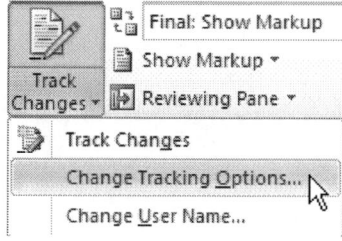

---

b. In the **Track Changes Options** dialog box, in the **Markup** section, to the right of the **Insertions** drop-down list, in the **Color** drop-down list, scroll down and select **Green.**

c. To the right of the **Deletions** drop-down list, click the **Color** drop-down, scroll down and select **Red.**

d. From the **Comments** drop-down list, select **Turquoise.**

e. In the **Balloons** section, in the **Use Balloons (Print and Web Layout)** drop-down list, verify that the **Only for comments/formatting** option is selected and click **OK.**

3. Review the document.

a. Click the **Track Changes** drop-down and choose **Track Changes.**

b. In the document, in the second line, select the text "continued strong" and type *booming.*

c. In the first bullet point, double-click the text "six" to select it and type *eleven.*

d. On the **Review** tab, in the **Comments** group, click **New Comment** and type *It's almost an eleven-fold increase.*

e. In the third bullet point, select the text "$10.7 million."

f. On the **Review** tab, in the **Comments** group, click **New Comment** and type *Is this correct?*

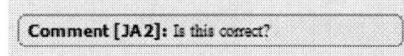

g. Save the document as *My Milestones* and close it.

Comments stays on after finalizing document

ACTIVITY 2-4
Modifying and Deleting Comments

Data Files:

C:\084584Data\Collaborating on Documents\Modified Milestones.docx

Scenario:

You reviewed a document and sent it to its author suggesting a few modifications. The author has sent it back to you for validation after making those changes.

---

1. Delete the comments.

    a. From the C:\084584Data\Collaborating on Documents folder, open the Modified Milestones.docx file.

    b. Place the insertion point at the end of the first comment.

    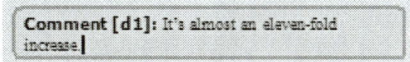
    Comment [d1]: It's almost an eleven-fold increase

    c. On the **Review** tab, in the **Comments** group, click **Delete.**

    d. Place the insertion point at the end of the last comment.

    e. On the **Review** tab, in the **Comments** group, click **Delete.**

---

2. Modify the comment inserted for the second bullet point.

    a. Triple-click the comment inserted for the second bullet point and type *I suggest you include the debt amount.*

    b. Save the document as *My Modified Milestones* and close it.

TOPIC D
Compare Document Changes

You tracked changes as you edited a document. However, when you have the original document and an edited copy, it can be difficult to identify subtle changes that have been made. In this topic, you will compare one document with another to clearly identify the changes between them.

The **Track Changes** option enables you to keep track of the changes made to a document. But, when the reviewer reviews a document without tracking the changes, you have to painstakingly compare the two documents manually, placing them side by side. Word provides an efficient method for comparing documents.

The Window Group

The **Window** group has a number of options that can be used for arranging, sizing, and managing multiple application windows.

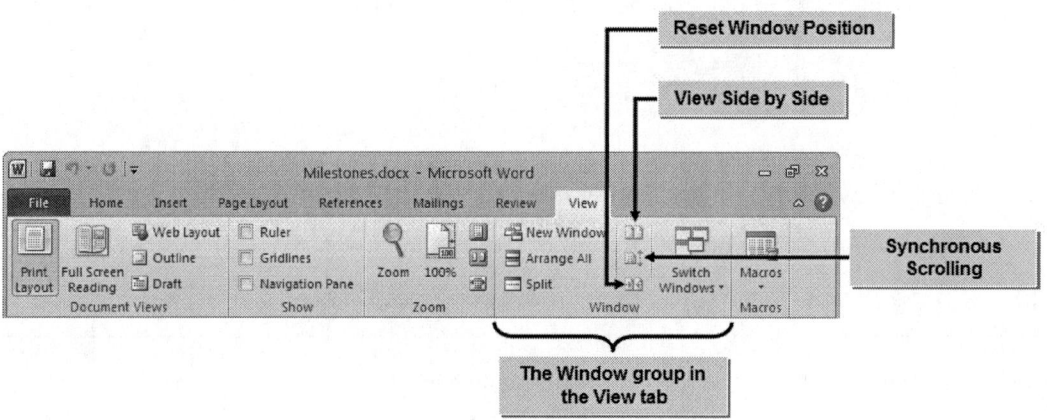

Figure 2-3: Options available in the Window group.

Option	Description
New Window	Used to display a document in a new window.
Arrange All	Used to tile all open windows horizontally.
Split	Used to split a window into multiple resizable panes to view different parts of a document.
View Side by Side	Used to view documents side-by-side for comparison.
Synchronous Scrolling	Used to synchronize the scrolling of documents that are displayed side-by-side.
Reset Window Position	Used to reset the window position of documents that are being compared by sharing the screen equally.
Switch Windows	Used to switch between open windows.

The Compare Documents Dialog Box

The options in the **Compare Documents** dialog box allow you to compare two versions of a document.

Option	Description
Original document drop-down list	Enables you to select the original document.
Revised document drop-down list	Enables you to select the updated or revised document.
More button	Displays the advanced formatting options spread across two sections.
	• The **Comparison settings** section: This section contains options for displaying or hiding the various changes made to the documents.
	• The **Show changes** section: This section allows you to select where you want to view the compared changes—in the original, revised, or new document. You also have the option to observe the changes at the character or word level.

Legal Blackline

The purpose of *Legal Blackline* is to identify the differences between two similar-looking documents. Markup options display the differences in a new document, though neither of the documents being compared is affected. You can enable the feature by selecting **Compare two versions of a document (legal blackline)**, in the **Compare** group, on the **Review** tab.

How to Compare Document Changes

Procedure Reference: Compare Documents

To compare documents:

1. Open the documents you want to compare.
2. On the **View** tab, in the **Window** group, click **View Side by Side.**
3. If necessary, in the **Compare Side by Side** dialog box, select the document to be compared.
4. If necessary, click **Reset Window Position** to position the windows side by side.
5. In either document, scroll up or down using the vertical scroll bar to browse the documents simultaneously and compare them.

 If the documents don't scroll together, on the **View** tab, in the **Window** group, click **Synchronous Scrolling.**

6. If necessary, make changes to the open documents.
7. If necessary, click **View Side by Side** to disable the option and display the documents separately.

Procedure Reference: Compare Document Changes

To compare document changes:

1. On the **Review** tab, in the **Compare** group, click **Compare** and choose **Compare.**

2. In the **Compare Documents** dialog box, select the original document.

   - From the **Original Document** drop-down list, select the desired document.

   - From the **Original Document** drop-down list, select **Browse** and navigate to and select the desired document.

   - Or, next to the **Original Document** drop-down list, click the **Browse** button and navigate to and select the desired document.

3. Select the revised document that you want to compare with the original document.

   - From the **Revised Document** drop-down list, select the desired document.

   - From the **Revised Document** drop-down list, select **Browse** and navigate to and select the desired document.

   - Or, next to the **Revised Document** drop-down list, click the **Browse** button and navigate to and select the desired document.

4. If necessary, select the document in which the changes need to be displayed.

   a. Click **More.**

   b. In the **Comparison settings** section, check or uncheck the desired option to hide or display the changes made based on the chosen option.

   c. In the **Show changes** section, in the **Show changes at** subsection, select the desired option.

      - Select **Character level** to display the changes at character level.

      - Select **Word level** to display the changes at word level.

   d. In the **Show changes in** section, select the desired option.

      - Select **Original document** to display the changes in the source document.

      - Select **Revised document** to display the changes in the edited document.

      - Or, select **New document** to display the changes in a new document.

5. Click **OK** to view the compared changes in the selected document.

Good!

ACTIVITY 2-5
Comparing Document Changes

Data Files:

C:\084584Data\Collaborating on Documents\Edited Milestones.docx, C:\084584Data\
Collaborating on Documents\Edited Milestones Tm.docx

Before You Begin:

Open a blank document.

Scenario:

You sent the Edited Milestones document to Tim Mahoney for review and he has sent back the document with his changes. Upon opening the document, you realize that he didn't enable track changes, so it isn't readily apparent what changes were made. You now need to figure out where he made the changes in the document.

1.   Compare the original document with the revised one.

   a.   On the **Review** tab, in the **Compare** group, click the **Compare** drop-down and choose **Compare**.

   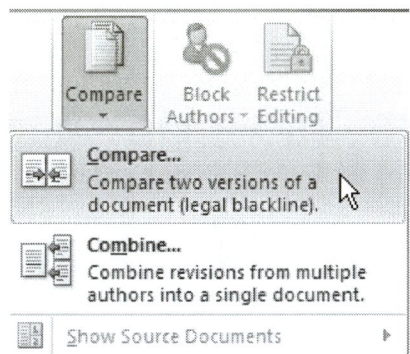

   b.   In the **Compare Documents** dialog box, in the **Original document** section, click the Browse button.

   c.   If necessary, in the **Open** dialog box, navigate to the C:\084584Data\Collaborating on Documents folder.

   d.   Open the Edited Milestones.docx file.

   e.   In the **Compare Documents** dialog box, in the **Revised document** section, click the Browse button.

   f.   Open the Edited Milestones Tm.docx file and in the **Compare Documents** dialog box, click **More**.

g. In the **Show changes** section, in the **Show changes in** subsection, verify that **New document** is selected by default and click **OK.**

> Show changes in:
> ○ Original document
> ○ Revised document
> ● New document

h. Observe that the changes made to the original document are tracked in a new document.

i. Save the document as *My Edited Milestones Tm* and close the document.

---

2. **True or False? The View Side by Side option allows you to tile horizontally all open windows.**

___ True

___ False

TOPIC E
Merge Document Changes

You identified the changes between two documents. Now, you may want to combine those changes into a single document. In this topic, you will merge changes from multiple documents.

Entering all changes made by multiple reviewers into the original document manually would take several hours of uninterrupted work. With Word, you can quickly merge all changes into a document, enabling you to begin reviewing the changes immediately.

The Combine Documents Dialog Box

The **Combine Documents** dialog box enables you to combine two different documents into one. The original and revised document drop-down lists allow you to specify the names of the original and revised documents, respectively. You can also set the comparison settings and choose whether you want the changes to be combined in the original, revised, or new document.

How to Merge Document Changes

Procedure Reference: Merge Document Changes

To merge document changes:

1. On the **Review** tab, in the **Compare** group, click **Compare** and choose **Combine.**
2. In the **Combine Documents** dialog box, select the original document.
3. In the **Combine Documents** dialog box, select the document that contains the changes you want to combine with the original document.
4. If necessary, click **More** to select the settings in which the changes need to be displayed.
5. Click **OK** to view the compared changes in the selected document.

 If you wish to merge multiple copies into the current document, repeat the steps as needed.

Track Changes in a Combined Document

When you combine two versions of a document, changes can be tracked in a combined document. The options in the Tracking group, on the Review tab, can be used to display the tracked changes as desired. The tracked changes can also be accepted or rejected to suit your requirements, to arrive at a final version of the combined document.

ACTIVITY 2-6
Merging Document Changes

Data Files:

C:\084584Data\Collaborating on Documents\Edited Management Team.docx, C:\084584Data\ Collaborating on Documents\Team Mc.docx, C:\084584Data\Collaborating on Documents\Team Sr.docx

Scenario:

You have received marked up copies of a document from multiple reviewers. You find it tedious to incorporate their changes one at a time.

---

1.   Merge the Team Mc.docx file with the Edited Management Team.docx file.

   a.   On the **Review** tab, in the **Compare** group, click the **Compare** drop-down and choose **Combine.**

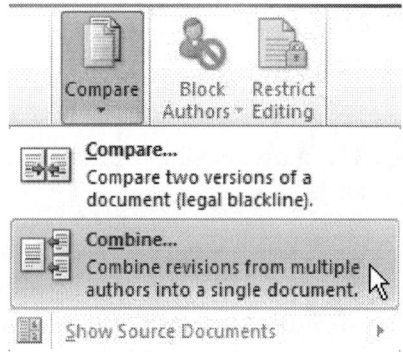

   b.   In the **Combine Documents** dialog box, in the **Original document** section, click the Browse button.

   c.   In the **Open** dialog box, open the Edited Management Team.docx file.

   d.   In the **Revised document** section, click the Browse button and open the Team Mc.docx file.

   e.   In the **Show changes** section, in the **Show changes in** subsection, select the **Original document** option and click **OK.**

   f.   Save the combined document as *My Edited Management Team*

---

2.   Merge the Team Sr.docx file with the My Edited Management Team.docx file.

   a.   Display the **Combine Documents** dialog box.

   b.   In the **Combine Documents** dialog box, in the **Original document** section, click the Browse button and open My Edited Management Team.docx.

   c.   In the **Revised document** section, click the Browse button and open Team Sr.docx.

d.   In the **Show changes** section, in the **Show changes in** subsection, verify that the **Original document** option is selected and click **OK.**

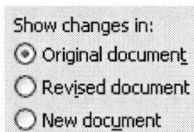

e.   Notice that the middle pane displays the combined changes in the My Edited Management Team document.

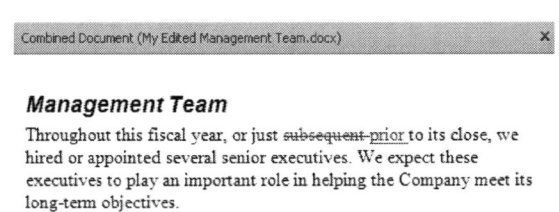

f.   Save the document and close all open documents.

TOPIC F

Review Track Changes and Comments

You have compared and merged all the tracked changes into a single document. However, not all reviewer changes are necessary, some may even conflict with other collaboration remarks. In this topic, you will accept and reject changes made to a document before sending out the final version.

Reviewing the tracked changes enables you to consider each suggestion or change and gives you the ability to accept or reject the suggested changes. This systematic approach also helps to ensure that you don't accidentally miss any markups no matter how small they are.

The Full Screen Reading View

The **Full Screen Reading** view allows you to increase or decrease the text size of a document without affecting its text formatting or page setup, so that it is easy to read and review the document on-screen.

View Options

The **Full Screen Reading** toolbar provides you with quick access to all tools necessary to make it easier for you to read or review a document on-screen. The **View Options** menu on the toolbar contains options relating to the display of pages and markup of the document.

Option	Used To
Don't Open Attachments in Full Screen	Restrict attachments opened from email applications or the SharePoint server from getting displayed in the **Full Screen Reading** view.
Increase Text Size/ Decrease Text Size	Increase or decrease the text size for easy reading.
Show One Page/Show Two Pages	Specify the number of pages to be displayed at a time.
Show Printed Page	Display the pages as they would look when printed. This option is similar to the print preview in Microsoft Word.
Margin Settings	Show, hide, or suppress margins on a printed page.
Allow Typing	Enable editing of the document in the **Full Screen Reading** view.
Track Changes	Enable track changes, specify the track change preferences, and change the reviewer's name and initials.
Show Comments And Changes	Select the type of markup to be displayed—comments, ink annotations, insertions and deletions, formatting, and markup area highlight. You can also choose to display changes and comments from specific reviewer(s).
Show Original/Final Document	Select whether you want to view the original or final document. You also have the option to view either of them with or without the changes.

The Navigation Pane

The **Navigation** pane appears to the left of the document and allows the user to quickly navigate to the desired location. It displays the headings and subheadings of the contents in the document, pages in the document, and the results from your current search.

How to Review Track Changes and Comments

Procedure Reference: Review Tracked Changes in the Full Screen Reading View

To review tracked changes in the **Full Screen Reading** view:

1. Switch to the **Full Screen Reading** view.

    ●   On the **View** tab, in the **Document Views** group, click **Full Screen Reading.**

    ●   Or, in the Microsoft Office status bar, click **Full Screen Reading.**

     If the document you want to review was sent to other mail recipients for review, you should click **End Review** on the **Reviewing** toolbar to indicate that the review stage has ended.

2. On the toolbar, click the **Jump to a page or section in the document** drop-down and choose **Navigation Pane** to display the **Navigation** pane and navigate to a particular section or page of the document.

3. If necessary, position the mouse pointer over a marked up instance or a comment to identify the reviewer responsible for the change.

4. If necessary, show or hide comments from individual reviewers.

    a.   In the **Full Screen** window, from the **View Options** drop-down, choose **Show Comments and Changes→Reviewers.**

    b.   Check a reviewer's name to show his or her comments, or uncheck reviewers whose comments you wish to hide.

Procedure Reference: Review Tracked Changes in the Print Layout View

To review tracked changes in the **Print Layout** view:

1. On the **Review** tab, in the **Tracking** group, click **Show Markup.** Choose **Reviewers** and then select the desired reviewer from the list to display comments from a specific reviewer.

2. Respond to a comment.

    a.   Place the insertion point in the comment balloon.

    b.   Insert a comment.

     Your comment will contain the letter "R" in the comment balloon where your initials are displayed, indicating that it is a response.

    c.   Type your text in the comment balloon.

3. Accept or reject the tracked changes and comments.

   a. If necessary, place the insertion point at the desired location in the document.

   b. On the **Review** tab, in the **Changes** group, click **Previous** or **Next** to move to the desired tracked change.

   c. Accept or reject the change.

      ● In the **Changes** group, click **Accept** to allow the insertion or deletion made to the document.

 When you accept a change that has a corresponding comment, you have the option of either retaining the comment by accepting it, or deleting it using the **Reject** button.

      ● Or, in the **Changes** group, click **Reject** to disallow the insertion or deletion made to the document.

 When you reject a change, both the change and the comment are deleted.

Procedure Reference: View Comments Inline and in Balloons

To view comments inline and in balloons:

1. Open a document with comments, or add comments to an open document.

2. On the **Review** tab, in the **Tracking** group, from the **Show Markup** drop-down list, select **Balloons** and then select the desired option.

   ● Select **Show All Revisions Inline** to view the comments inline.

   ● Select **Show All Revisions Balloons** to view the comments in balloons.

ACTIVITY 2-7
Reviewing the Tracked Changes and Comments

Data Files:

C:\084584Data\Collaborating on Documents\Review Management Team.docx

Scenario:

With all the changes merged into the Review Management Team document, you now need to review the changes and accept or reject them, as needed.

---

1. Preview the document changes in the Full Screen Reading view.

   a. From the C:\084584Data\Collaborating on Documents folder, open the Review Management Team.docx file.

   b. On the **View** tab, in the **Document Views** group, click **Full Screen Reading** to switch to the Full Screen Reading view.

   c. On the toolbar, click the **Jump to a page or section in the document** drop-down and select **Navigation Pane.**

   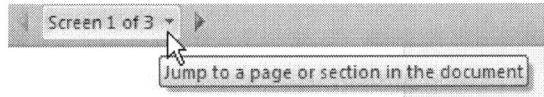

   d. In the document, observe the green headings that indicate inserted text.

   e. In the **Navigation** pane, click **Talent** to display the relevant content on page four.

   f. Click **Management Team** to return to the beginning of the document.

   g. In the **Navigation** pane, select the **Browse the pages in your document** tab.

   h. Observe that the comment balloons and markups are visible, but not legible. Verify that the first thumbnail is selected.

   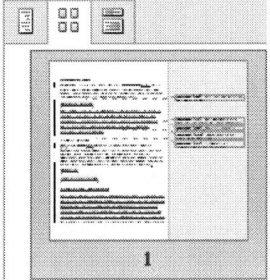

---

2. Hide Justine Altman's comment as it is not pertinent to the review.

   a. On the toolbar, from the **View Options** drop-down menu, choose **Show Comments and Changes→Reviewers.**

---

b. Uncheck Justine Altman from the list.

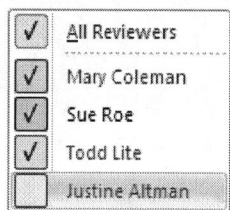

c. In the document, observe that the comment with the author **JA2** is not visible.

d. Click **Close** to return to **Print Layout** view.

3. Review the changes.

a. On the **Review** tab, in the **Changes** group, click **Accept**.

b. Notice that the word "subsequent" is selected. In the **Changes** group, click **Accept**.

c. Notice that the word "prior" is selected. Click **Accept** to accept the change.

d. Observe that the "Relocation Services" paragraph is selected. In the **Changes** group, click **Reject**.

e. Notice that both the inserted text and the comment have been deleted.

f. Accept the deletion of the name "Joan."

g. Accept the insertion of the name "John."

h. Notice that the comment corresponding to the word "John" is highlighted. Click **Reject** to delete the comment.

i. Delete the comment **MC2**.

j. Reject the "Today's Opportunities" insertion made by Todd.

k. In the **Microsoft Word** message box, click **Show All** to start searching from the beginning of the document.

4. Respond to Justine Altman's comment.

a. Observe that Justine Altman's comment is displayed. In the **Comments** group, click **New Comment**.

b. Observe that a new comment balloon is displayed with an "R" after your user name to indicate it is a response. Type **Names have been confirmed.**

c. Save the document as **My Review Management Team** and close it.

TOPIC G
Coauthor a Document

So far, you have collaborated with your reviewers in an asynchronous mode. Word provides you with advanced features that facilitate real-time synchronized coauthoring capabilities and work on documents over the web. In this topic, you will simultaneously work on a document with your reviewer and edit documents over the web.

When you are asked to send a document for review immediately, and you feel that there are some minor modifications to be made to the document, you can go ahead and send the document for review, while you can still work on the same document and enhance it. Word provides you with the coauthoring feature that enables you to simultaneously edit the same document with multiple resources and also keep track of the changes–all in real time.

Coauthoring

Coauthoring is a Word 2010 feature that enables you to work simultaneously with others on a document. It displays the changes made to the document and the author who made them. The changes are displayed when you save the document. A small icon appears on the status bar of the application indicating the number of people working on the document. When you click on a particular author's name, you can see the person's availability and contact information. For coauthoring to work, you require SharePoint Foundation 2010, Microsoft® Office SharePoint® Server, or a Windows Live ID. Also, when combined with Microsoft Office Communications Server, you can initiate conversations with editors and reviewers.

Microsoft Office Communicator

Microsoft Office Communicator is an instant messaging client that enables users to communicate and collaborate online from different locations. You can also make phone calls, video conferences, share desktop, documents, and other files.

Microsoft® Office SharePoint® Server 2010

Microsoft® Office SharePoint® Server 2010 is a collaboration and content management server integrated with the Office 2010 suite. It acts as a repository where files can be saved and accessed from different locations. The SharePoint server tracks the work done on a file by maintaining information on users and file versions. The server also acts as a common platform for hosting content on the Internet and intranet. In addition, the SharePoint server can be used to control access and content modification permissions for files stored on the server.

Microsoft Office SharePoint Server 2010 vs. Microsoft SharePoint Foundation 2010

Similar to Microsoft Office SharePoint Server 2010, *Microsoft SharePoint Foundation 2010* is also a collaboration software product from Microsoft that provides a central location for individuals working in a project team or functional group to share information and communicate with one another. It provides specialized websites that contain elements, including a central calendar; task lists; discussion boards; wikis; blogs; and libraries of documents, photos, and forms. Microsoft SharePoint Foundation 2010 is suited for small teams and projects, whereas Microsoft Office SharePoint Server 2010 is an enterprise-level server with additional functionalities, such as advanced search capabilities and personalized sites for users to share information.

Word Web App

Word Web App is an application that can be accessed online by using a web browser. It provides the same functionality as Word 2010. You can access Word Web App by using a SkyDrive account or on Microsoft SharePoint 2010. You can also view, edit, or coauthor documents, and the changes made to a document are automatically saved by Word Web App. You can use the Windows Live feature integrated with the SkyDrive application to store and review documents over the web, without the need for an Office application running on your system.

The Save to Windows Live Feature

Word 2010 allows you to save your documents directly to the web using your Windows Live SkyDrive account. It provides 25 GB of online space to store your documents, and enables you to access the documents from any computer at any location. Using the **Save to Windows Live** feature, you can view, edit, or download documents, create and share multiple folders, set permissions on folders, add comments in documents, and track versions of documents.

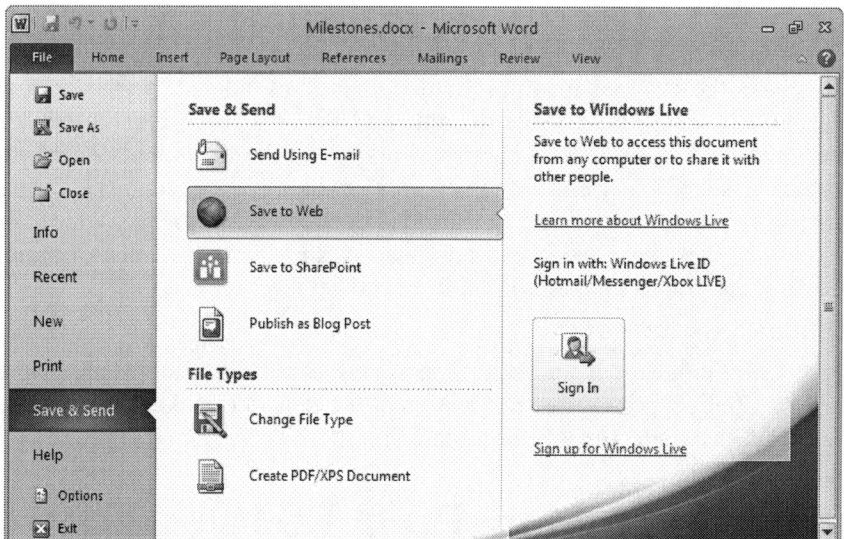

Figure 2-4: *The Save to Windows Live option allows you to save documents to the web.*

Windows Live SkyDrive

Windows Live SkyDrive is a service provided by Microsoft that allows users with a Windows Live ID to store and share files on the web.

How to Coauthor a Document

Procedure Reference: Coauthor Documents Using Microsoft Office SharePoint Server

To coauthor documents using Microsoft Office SharePoint Server:

1. In the address bar of the browser window, type the URL of your SharePoint site and click **Go** to open the SharePoint web page.

2. On the **Home** page, in the **Shared Documents** section, click **Add document** to browse for the document you want to add to SharePoint.

3. In the **Upload Document** dialog box, in the **Name** text box, click **Browse** to add the path of the desired file.

4. If necessary, in the **Version Comments** text area, type comments about the document you are about to add.

5. Disable the **Require Check Out** option to avoid checking out the document for editing.

   a. On the **Library Tools Library** contextual tab, in the **Settings** group, click **Library Settings** to open the settings page.

   b. In the **General Settings** section, click **Versioning settings** to disable the option to modify the document settings.

   c. In the **Require Check Out** section, in the right pane, select **No** and click **OK** to disable the **Require Check Out** option.

6. In the left pane, in the **Libraries** section, click **Shared Documents.**

7. On the **Shared Documents** page, move the mouse pointer over the added file name to display its check box. Check the file name.

8. On the **Library Tools Documents** contextual tab, in the **Share & Track** group, click **E-mail a Link** to share the document with others using Microsoft Outlook.

9. If necessary, in the **Internet Explorer Security** window, click **Allow** to let Internet Explorer open web content using Microsoft Outlook.

10. If necessary, configure the settings of Microsoft Outlook.

    a. In the **Microsoft Outlook 2010 Startup** dialog box, click **Next** twice.

    b. In the **E-mail Account** section, select **Manually configure server settings or additional server types** and click **Next** twice.

    c. In the **User Information** section, type your name and E-mail address in the corresponding text boxes.

    d. In the **Server Information** section, enter the desired account type and mail server information.

    e. In the **Logon Information** section, type your user name and password with which you want to log in.

    f. Click **Finish** to open Microsoft Outlook.

11. In the Microsoft Outlook window, in the **To** text box, enter the email addresses of people with whom you want to share the document.

12. In the **Subject** text box, enter the text that you want to appear as the subject in the email, and click **Send.**

13. In the browser window, in the **Shared Documents** section, click the file name that you have checked already.

14. In the **Open Document** dialog box, select **Edit** and click **OK** to open the document using Microsoft Word.

15. If necessary, in the **User Name** dialog box, enter the desired user name and initials and click **OK.**

16. In the Word document, make the necessary changes, and in the Quick Access toolbar, click the **Save** button to display the changes to others who are working on the same document and to view the changes made by others.

17. If necessary, as a coauthoring partner, open the document and edit the contents.

    a. Open Microsoft Outlook, and in the inbox, click the link sent by the other user to open the document.

    b. In the Word window, in the message bar, click **Edit Document.**

    c. In the Word document, make the necessary changes, and in the Quick Access toolbar, click the **Save** button to display the changes to others who are working on the same document and to view the changes made by others.

18. If necessary, on the status bar, click the icon that appears next to the **Proofing errors** icon to view the authors who are editing the document.

Procedure Reference: Save a Document to Windows Live SkyDrive

To save a document to Windows Live SkyDrive:

1. On the **File** tab, select **Save & Send.**

2. In the **Save & Send** section, click **Save to Web.**

3. In the **Save to Windows Live** section, click **Sign In** and enter your Windows Live or Hotmail credentials.

4. In the **My Folders** section, choose the folder where you want to save the document in and click **Save As.**

5. In the **Save As** dialog box, enter a name for the document and click **Save.**

Procedure Reference: Coauthor Documents Using Windows Live SkyDrive

To coauthor documents using Windows Live SkyDrive:

1. In the address bar of your browser window, type **http://skydrive.live.com.**

2. Enter your Windows Live login credentials.

3. On the Windows Live window, browse to the document you want to share.

4. From the SkyDrive menu, click the **Share** drop-down and choose **Edit permissions** to change the permissions of a document.

5. In the **Add specific people** section, in the **Enter a name or an e-mail address** text box, enter the email address of the person to whom you want to grant full access to the shared document, and click **Save** to set permissions.

6. In the **Send a notification** section, click **Send.**

7. In the menu, click the **Share** drop-down and choose **Send a link.**

8. On the **Send a link** page, in the **To** text box, enter the email address of the person whom you want to share the document with and click **Send.**

9. Click the file that you want to coauthor.

10. On the Microsoft Word Web App page, from the menu, click **Open in Word.**

 You can also edit the document directly in the browser window by clicking the **Edit in Browser** link.

11. If necessary, in the **Open Document** dialog box, click **OK.**

12. In the Connecting to .docs.live.net dialog box, enter your Windows Live email address and password in the respective text boxes.

13. In the Word document, make the necessary changes, and in the Quick Access toolbar, click the **Save** button to display the changes to others who are working on the same document and to view the changes made by others.

14. As a coauthoring partner, open the document and edit the contents.

    a. Log in to SkyDrive using your Windows Live or Hotmail log in credentials.

    b. On the top of the SkyDrive page, click **Hotmail** to open the inbox.

    c. Navigate to the mail sent by the other user, and in the mail, click **View folder.**

    d. If necessary, in the **Message from webpage** dialog box, click **OK.**

    e. Click the file that you want to coauthor.

    f. On the Microsoft Word Web App page, from the Word Web App menu bar, click **Open in Word.**

    g. If necessary, in the **Open Document** dialog box, click **OK.**

    h. In the Connecting to .docs.live.net dialog box, enter your Windows Live or Hotmail email address and password in the respective text boxes.

    i. If necessary, in the Word document, in the message bar, click **Enable Editing.**

    j. In the Word document, make the necessary changes, and in the Quick Access toolbar, click the **Save** button to display the changes to others who are working on the same document and to view the changes made by others.

DISCOVERY ACTIVITY 2-8
Coauthoring a Document

Data Files:

C:\084584Data\Collaborating on Documents\Simulations\Coauthoring a Document_guided.exe

Setup:

This is a simulated activity. In this simulation, SharePoint Foundation 2010 has been installed with the following URL: **http://dc**

Scenario:

Your manager wants to review the Milestones.docx file; he asks you to mail the document immediately. You still have some changes to make; therefore, you share the document with your manager and make the necessary changes simultaneously.

---

1. To launch the simulation, browse to the C:\084584Data\Collaborating on Documents\ Simulations folder.

---

2. Double-click the Coauthoring a Document_guided.exe file.

---

3. Maximize the simulation window.

---

4. Follow the onscreen steps for the simulation.

---

5. When you have finished the activity, close the simulation window.

Lesson 2 Follow-up

In this lesson, you shared, reviewed, and tracked changes in a Word document in a collaborative environment. With advanced tracking, commenting, and coauthoring features, you can streamline and manage your review and collaboration tasks effectively.

1. **How will you use Word to collaborate on documents?**

2. **What types of documents have you been asked to collaborate on in your daily work?**

3 | Managing Document Versions

Lesson Time: 30 minutes

Lesson Objectives:

In this lesson, you will manage document versions.

You will:

- Create a new document version.
- Compare document versions.
- Merge document versions.

Introduction

In the previous lesson, you collaborated on documents. When a document goes through the collaboration process, multiple versions of the document are created. In this lesson, you will manage document versions.

Your document may go through many rounds of reviews, resulting in the creation of multiple versions. Managing different document versions can be made a lot easier and less prone to errors with the use of a central document repository.

TOPIC A

Create a New Document Version

You reviewed changes and comments in a document that were tracked in Word. You wish to update the document and also retain the original version. In this topic, you will create a new document version.

There may be times when you want to save changes to a document without overwriting it. Saving your modified documents with different file names can lead to confusion and errors. Microsoft® Office SharePoint® Server 2010, a collaboration and content management server, enables you to manage versions of a document and even restore an earlier version of the document.

Versioning

Definition:

Versioning is the process of recording and storing changes made to a document over the course of its development. Each time the document is checked in to the server, all changes since the previous version are also stored in the current document. As file versions accumulate, you can revisit, review, or reuse any of the versions.

Example:

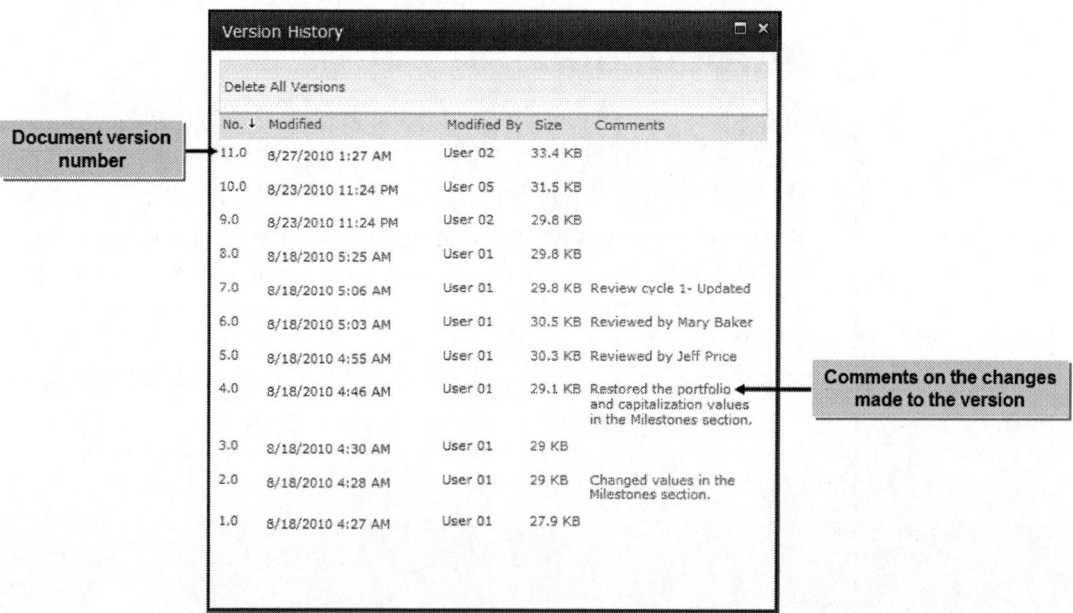

Figure 3-1: Versions of a document in Microsoft Office SharePoint Server 2010.

Versioning Settings

The **Versioning Settings** page provides you with options that help control the versioning of documents you want to share using the SharePoint server.

Section	Allows You To
Content Approval	Specify if the edited content of a document requires approval before it is saved as a version.
Document Version History	Enable or disable versioning. If enabled, you can specify whether you want to create a major version for every edited document or save a version as draft—a minor version—until the edited content is approved. You can also specify the number of versions you want to retain for a document.
Draft Item Security	Control who can view the draft copies of a document in the document library.
Require Check Out	Specify whether users must check out documents before they can make changes to the document in the document library.

Major vs. Minor Versions

Versions are classified as either major (for example, adding, changing, or deleting large sections of text) or minor (for example, updating a few figures in a spreadsheet or changing the wording of a sentence). Major versions are indicated by whole numbers (1.0, 2.0, 3.0, etc.), while minor versions are indicated by decimals (1.1, 1.2, 1.3, etc.).

How to Create a New Document Version

Procedure Reference: Specify the Versioning Settings in a SharePoint Site

To specify the versioning settings in a SharePoint site:

1. On the **Home** page of the document workspace, click the **Shared Documents** link.
2. On the **Shared Documents** page, on the **Library Tools Library** contextual tab, in the **Settings** group, click **Library Settings.**
3. On the **Document Library Settings** page, in the **General Settings** section, click the **Versioning settings** link.
4. On the **Versioning Settings** page, specify the appropriate versioning settings.
5. Click **OK** to save the changes made.

Procedure Reference: Upload a Document to SharePoint

To upload a document to the SharePoint server:

1. On the **Shared Documents** page of the server, click the **Add Documents** link to upload a document to the document library.
2. In the **Upload Document** dialog box, click **Browse.**
3. In the **Choose File** dialog box, click the **Browse** button to browse to the location of the file that you want to upload.
4. Select the file and then click **Open.**

5. In the **Shared Documents** dialog box, in the **Edit** tab, in the **Commit** group, click **Check In.**

6. If necessary, in the **Version Comments** text box, add a comment describing the document.

7. Click **OK** to upload the file.

Procedure Reference: Upload Multiple Documents to SharePoint

To upload multiple documents to the SharePoint server:

1. On the **Shared Documents** page of the server, click the **Add Documents** link to upload a document to the document library.

2. In the **Upload Document** dialog box, click the **Upload Multiple Files** link.

3. In the **Upload Multiple Documents** dialog box, click the **Browse for files instead** to browse to the location of the files that you want to upload.

 You can also drag files and folders into the **Upload Multiple Documents** dialog box.

4. Select the files, click **Open** and click **OK** to upload the file.

Procedure Reference: Check Out and Check In a Document Using the SharePoint Server

To check out and check in a document using the SharePoint server:

1. Check out a document using the SharePoint server.

   a. Navigate to the document library that contains the document you want to check out.

 If you have just checked in the document, you may have to refresh the web page to update the menu options.

   b. Place the mouse pointer over the document you want to check out, and from the drop-down menu for the document, click **Check Out.**

   c. In the **Microsoft Internet Explorer** message box that indicates that you are about to check out the specified document, check the **Use my local drafts folder** check box and then click **OK.**

   d. In the **Shared Documents** section, a green box with an arrow appears near the Word 2010 file icon to indicate that the document has been checked out.

   e. If necessary, navigate to the location where the checked-out files are saved and open and make the necessary changes to the document.

 Use the options in the **Save** tab of the **Word Options** dialog box to specify where you want to save the checked-out files from your document management server. By default, files are saved to the **SharePoint Drafts** folder in **My Documents.**

2. Check in the document using the SharePoint server.

    a. Navigate to the library that holds the document you have checked out.

    b. Place the mouse pointer over the document you want to check in, and from the drop-down menu for the document, click **Check In.**

    c. If necessary, on the **Check In** page, in the **Comments** text box, type your comments on the changes made to the version.

    d. Click **OK** to check in the document.

 Every time a document is checked in, SharePoint maintains a version of the changes made to the document since the previous version.

Procedure Reference: Check Out and Check In a Document Using Word 2010

To check out and check in a document using Word 2010:

1. Check out a document using Word 2010.

    a. Open a document that is to be checked out from the SharePoint site in Microsoft Word.

    b. In the **Open Document** dialog box, click **OK** to open the document.

 The document opens from the server in the read only mode.

    c. Check out the document.

    ● Add the **Server** button to the Quick Access toolbar. From the **Server** drop-down, select **Check Out.**

    ● Or, on the **File** tab, in the center pane, in the **Versions and Check Out** section, click the **Manage Versions** drop-down and select **Check Out.**

    d. Make the necessary changes to the document.

2. Check in the document using Word 2010.

    a. Check in the document.

    ■ Add the **Server** button to the Quick Access toolbar. From the **Server** drop-down, select **Check In.**

    ■ Or, on the **File** tab, in the center pane, in the **Checked Out Document** section, click **Check In.**

    b. If necessary, in the **Check In** dialog box, in the **Version Comments** text box, type your comments on the changes made to the version.

    c. Click **OK** to check in the document.

Procedure Reference: View the Version History of a Document

To view the version history of a document:

1. Open the document from the SharePoint server for which you want to view the version history.

2. If necessary, add the **Server** command to the Quick Access toolbar.

3. On the Quick Access toolbar, click **Server** and select **View Version History** to display the different versions of the document available in the **Versions saved for [File Name]** dialog box.

4. If necessary, in the **Comments** column, click a comment to view it completely in the **Check In Comments** message box and then click **Close.**

5. Select an option to work with the different versions displayed.

    ●   Select a version and click **Open** to recover the draft version of the document.

    ●   Select a version and click **Compare** to compare the selected version with the current version.

    ●   Select a version and click **Restore** to replace the current version of the document with the earlier version.

    ●   Select a version and click **Delete** to delete the draft version.

6. Click **Close** to close the dialog box.

Accessing Documents Directly from a SharePoint Site

Documents that are already saved in a SharePoint site can also be accessed by browsing to the SharePoint site. You can enter the URL to the workspace directly in your web browser. You can then check out, check in, and view the different versions of a document.

DISCOVERY ACTIVITY 3-1
Creating a New Document Version

Data Files:

C:\084584Data\Managing Document Versions\Creating a New Document Version_guided.exe

Setup:

This is a simulated activity. In this simulation, SharePoint Server 2010 has been installed with the following URL **http://dc** and multiple files have been uploaded to the server. You have been added to the SharePoint site and provided with full control permission. The versioning settings for the site are set to create major document versions and check out documents before making changes in the document library. In addition, the Server command has been added to the Quick Access toolbar.

Scenario:

Your company has decided to use SharePoint 2010 as its content management server. As you are part of the team developing content, your machine has been configured to the server and you are expected to start using it for your next project, which is the company's annual report. You have just completed the first draft and sent it to your manager. After a quick review, your manager asks you to change the increase in the net income, portfolio, and capitalization values in the Milestones section. You are doubtful about the changes, but because you are unable to clarify them right away, you decide to incorporate them anyway. You want to be able to access the original version in case you need it later.

---

1. To launch the simulation, navigate to the C:\084584Data\Managing Document Versions\ Simulations folder.

---

2. Double-click the Creating a New Document Version_guided.exe file.

---

3. Maximize the simulation window.

---

4. Follow the onscreen steps for the simulation.

---

5. When you have finished the activity, close the simulation window.

TOPIC B

Compare Document Versions

You have created versions of a document. You now need to identify the changes made to the latest version of the document in relation to the original document. In this topic, you will compare document versions.

You prepare a document and send it for review, only to receive the modified document a few days later without change tracking. You're having a hard time identifying those changes. Printing the latest version and the previous version of the document and comparing them manually is a painstaking process and can be error prone. Word provides a much more efficient method for comparing document versions.

How to Compare Document Versions

Procedure Reference: Compare Two Versions of a Document

To compare two versions of a document:

1. From the SharePoint server, check out the document you want to compare with a previous version of the document on the server.

2. On the **Review** tab, in the **Compare** group, click the **Compare** drop-down and select an option to compare multiple versions of a document.

    - Select **Major Version** to compare the document with its last major version published on the server.

    - Select **Last Version** to compare the document with the last version saved on the server.

    - Select **Specific Version** to compare the document with a specific version saved on the server.

The Compare Option

The options in the **Compare** drop-down will be listed only if the versioning settings for the document are turned on and if the document is opened from the SharePoint site.

DISCOVERY ACTIVITY 3-2
Comparing Two Versions of a Document

Data Files:

C:\084584Data\Managing Document Versions\Simulations\Comparing Two Versions of a Document_guided.exe

Setup:

This is a simulated activity. For this simulation, a SharePoint site with the URL **http://dc** has been created for your team with a document library. Multiple versions of the Annual Report document have been created in SharePoint for you.

Scenario:

After making changes to the annual report based on your manager's suggestions, you get a call from him stating that he was wrong about the portfolio and capitalization values and would like for you to retain their original values. You have been working on other reports lately, and do not recall the changes that were made.

---

1. To launch the simulation, navigate to the C:\084584Data\Managing Document Versions\ Simulations folder.

---

2. Double-click the Comparing Two Versions of a Document_guided.exe file.

---

3. Maximize the simulation window.

---

4. Follow the onscreen steps for the simulation.

---

5. When you have finished the activity, close the simulation window.

TOPIC C
Merge Document Versions

In the previous topic, you compared versions of a document. After having identified the changes made in different versions of the document, you may now need to combine them into a single document so that you can review them. In this topic, you will merge document versions.

Sometimes you may find yourself in a situation where your documents have been through multiple rounds of review. Consolidating a list of comments and other grammatical changes from all reviewers would be time consuming. Word provides you with a much more efficient option to merge changes made in different versions of a document into one document.

How to Merge Document Versions

Procedure Reference: Merge Multiple Versions of a Document

To merge multiple versions of a document:

1. From the SharePoint server, check out the document you want to merge.
2. Open the document versions that you want to merge.
   a. On the Quick Access toolbar, click the **Server** button and select **View Version History** to display the different versions of the document available in the **Versions saved for [File Name]** dialog box.
   b. Select the version and click **Open** to open the document.
3. On the **Review** tab, in the **Compare** group, click the **Compare** drop-down and select **Combine** to display the **Combine Documents** dialog box.
4. From the **Original document** drop-down list, select a version.

 To display a version as an option in the **Original document** and **Revised document** drop-down lists, you must first open the version of the document using the **Versions saved for [File Name]** dialog box.

5. From the **Revised document** drop-down list, select the version you want to combine with the original document.
6. If necessary, click **More,** and in the **Show changes in** section, select the option based on the document in which the combined changes need to be displayed.
7. Click **OK.**

 If the **Microsoft Office Word** dialog box appears, select the document for which you want to retain the formatting changes.

8. If necessary, save the document as a local copy or as a new document to the document library in your SharePoint server.

DISCOVERY ACTIVITY 3-3
Merging Multiple Versions of a Document

Data Files:

C:\084584Data\Managing Document Versions\Simulations\Merging Multiple Versions of a Document_guided.exe

Setup:

This is a simulated activity. For this simulation, a SharePoint site with the URL **http://dc** has been created for your team with a document library. Multiple versions of the Annual Report document have been created in SharePoint for you.

Scenario:

As a new employee, the annual report is the first official document you have been asked to work on. You would like to study the changes suggested by different reviewers in the previous versions of the report so that you can create a report that meets their requirements. However, there is a different version in SharePoint for each reviewer and you want to avoid having to look up each version.

---

1. To launch the simulation, navigate to the C:\084584Data\Managing Document Versions\ Simulations folder.

---

2. Double-click the **Merging Multiple Versions of a Document_guided.exe** file.

---

3. Maximize the simulation window.

---

4. Follow the on-screen steps for the simulation.

---

5. When you have finished the activity, close the simulation window.

Lesson 3 Follow-up

In this lesson, you managed different versions that were created automatically each time a document is checked into SharePoint Server 2010.

1. **What situations would require you to compare different document versions?**

2. **Why would you choose to merge different document versions?**

4 | Adding Reference Marks and Notes

Lesson Time: 1 hour(s), 15 minutes

Lesson Objectives:

In this lesson, you will add reference marks and notes.

You will:

- Insert bookmarks.

- Insert footnotes and endnotes.

- Add captions to illustrations.

- Add hyperlinks.

- Add cross-references.

- Add citations and a bibliography.

Introduction

You managed multiple versions of a document. The ability to mark specific locations in a document and provide additional descriptions will help you to build a convenient reference source. In this lesson, you will add reference marks and notes.

While working with large documents, it is always handy to include information on sources alongside content. Apart from enabling you to keep track of a source, references in a document provide supplemental information to your readers.

TOPIC A

Insert Bookmarks

You have completed work on your document. Now, you are ready to create references that make browsing through the document a lot easier. In this topic, you will insert bookmarks.

Scrolling through a long document to locate the information that you are looking for can be taxing and time consuming. By inserting bookmarks in long documents, you can avoid scrolling through the entire document trying to find a context. Bookmarks allow you to return directly to a location in the document where you want to reference a context.

Bookmarks

Bookmarks are markers within a document that enable you to quickly return to a given location. They can be used to mark important information or interesting facts in the document. In Word 2010, you can access the **Bookmark** option from the **Links** group on the **Insert** tab.

Other Uses of Bookmarks

Apart from using bookmarks to mark and locate important information in a document, you can use bookmarks for other purposes. You can insert a cross-reference to a bookmark's text, page number, and paragraph number. Also, you can insert a bookmarked portion of another document into the current document.

Bookmark Formatting Marks

When you insert a bookmark into a document, the bookmarked location is marked by the bookmark formatting mark. This mark can be displayed using the options in the **Word Options** dialog box. The bookmark formatting marks that appear vary based on the content being bookmarked. For instance, when you insert a bookmark for a specific location, the bookmark formatting mark is displayed as an I-beam. It appears as brackets when inserted for a selection.

The Bookmark Dialog Box

The **Bookmark** dialog box contains options that enable you to add, delete, or navigate to a bookmark in a document. In the **Sort by** section, you can choose to sort the list of available bookmarks by either name or location. You also have the option to display a list of hidden bookmarks in the **Bookmark name** list box.

Hidden Bookmarks

Hidden bookmarks are generally created by Word to mark certain fields in a document. They can also be created using Visual Basic for Applications (VBA), Visual Basic (VB), or other automation languages. These bookmarks are not indicated by bookmark formatting marks.

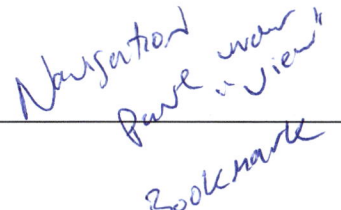

How to Insert Bookmarks

Procedure Reference: Insert Bookmarks

To insert bookmarks:

1. If necessary, display bookmark formatting marks.

   a. Open the **Word Options** dialog box.

   b. In the **Advanced** category, in the **Show document content** section, check **Show bookmarks.**

   c. Click **OK** to close the **Word Options** dialog box.

2. Select the location, section, or item where you want to insert the bookmark.

3. Display the **Bookmark** dialog box.

   ● On the **Insert** tab, in the **Links** group, click **Bookmark.**

   ● Or, press Ctrl+Shift+F5.

4. In the **Bookmark name** text box, type a name for the bookmark.

 While naming a bookmark, do not include spaces between words. Instead, use an underscore to indicate a space. For example, my_bookmark.

5. Click **Add** to insert the new bookmark.

6. If necessary, navigate to a bookmark.

   a. Display the **Bookmark** dialog box.

   b. Select a bookmark and click **Go To.**

7. If necessary, in the **Bookmark** dialog box, select the bookmark and click **Delete** to delete a bookmark.

8. Close the **Bookmark** dialog box.

Procedure Reference: Insert a Bookmarked Portion of a Document into the Current Document

To insert a bookmarked portion of a document into the current document:

1. Open the document in which you want to copy the bookmarked content.

2. Place the insertion point in a blank line after the text where you wish to include the bookmarked content.

3. On the **Insert** tab, in the **Text** group, click the **Object** drop-down arrow and choose **Text from File.**

4. In the **Insert File** dialog box, navigate to the file that contains the bookmarked content and click **Range.**

5. In the **Enter Text** dialog box, type the name of the bookmark you wish to insert and click **OK.**

6. In the **Insert File** dialog box, click **Insert.**

ACTIVITY 4-1
Using Bookmarks

Data Files:

C:\084584Data\Adding Reference Marks and Notes\Annual Report.docx

Scenario:

While working on the annual financial report, you realize that the content on page 10 is important and you may need to refer to this page several times. You want an easy method for navigating to that content rather than scrolling through the pages. You also find that the title "Financial Overview" has been bookmarked by another user. As you do not find the content important, you decide to remove the bookmark to keep your document neat and organized.

---

1. Display the bookmark formatting marks.

   a. From the C:\084584Data\Adding Reference Marks and Notes folder, open the Annual Report.docx file.

   b. On the **View** tab, check **Navigation Pane** to display the **Navigation** pane.

   c. Display the **Advanced** category in the **Word Options** dialog box.

   d. Scroll down, and in the **Show document content** section, check **Show bookmarks**.

   > **Show document content**
   >
   > ☐ Show background colors and images in Print Layout view
   > ☐ Show text wrapped within the document window
   > ☐ Show picture placeholders ⓘ
   > ☑ Show drawings and text boxes on screen
   > ☑ Show text animation
   > ☑ Show bookmarks

   e. Click **OK** to close the **Word Options** dialog box and display the bookmark formatting marks.

---

2. Bookmark the title "Talent."

   a. In the **Navigation** pane, click the **Browse the headings in your document** tab.

   b. Scroll down and click **Talent**.

   c. On the **Insert** tab, in the **Links** group, click **Bookmark**.

   d. In the **Bookmark** dialog box, in the **Bookmark name** text box, type *Talent* and click **Add.**

e. Notice that an I-beam is displayed near the text "Talent," indicating the presence of a bookmark.

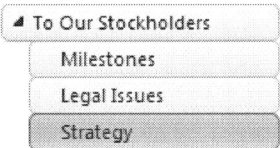

3. Bookmark the paragraph under "Strategy" on page 4 along with the graphic.

   a. In the **Navigation** pane, click **Strategy.**

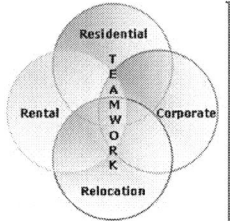

   b. Select the "Strategy" paragraph along with the graphic below it.

   c. Display the **Bookmark** dialog box.

   d. In the **Bookmark** dialog box, in the **Bookmark name** text box, type *Strategy* and click **Add.**

   e. Click near the graphic to deselect it.

   f. Notice that the title "Strategy" and the graphic below are enclosed in brackets.

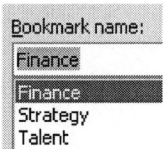

4. Delete the "Finance" bookmark.

   a. Display the **Bookmark** dialog box.

   b. In the **Bookmark name** list box, select **Finance** and click **Go To.**

c. Observe that you are taken to the bookmarked location. In the **Bookmark** dialog box, click **Delete.**

d. Click **Close** to close the **Bookmark** dialog box.

e. Notice that the bookmark formatting mark before the "Financial Overview" title has been removed, indicating that the bookmark has been deleted.

f. Save the file as ***My Annual Report***

TOPIC B
Insert Footnotes and Endnotes

You have inserted bookmarks for quick reference to specific content. In the course of your work, you may have referenced or reused thoughts or ideas presented by other authors. In this topic, you will insert footnotes and endnotes citing references to borrowed content.

When you intend to use some published article as source for your work, it is mandatory for you to credit the source. If you tend to neglect it and use someone else's work without giving them credit, you could find yourself in serious legal trouble. Properly citing the source in a footnote or an endnote can help you avoid such situations.

Footnotes and Endnotes

A *footnote* is a note that is inserted at the bottom of a page. It is associated with a particular term in the document and is used to provide additional information about that term or to cite references to the source of the term. It is always added to the same page as the text that is marked. *Endnotes* are similar to footnotes except that they are inserted at the end of a section. The note reference mark appearing after a relevant term and before a footnote or endnote indicates the connection between the two.

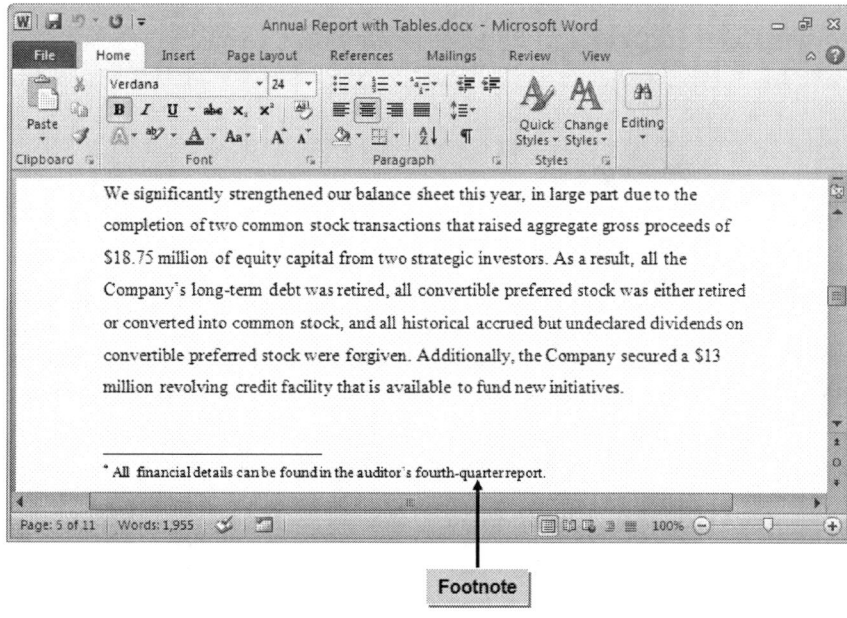

Figure 4-1: *Footnote inserted in a document.*

The Footnote and Endnote Dialog Box

The **Footnote and Endnote** dialog box contains three sections, each with options to add, format, and modify a footnote or an endnote.

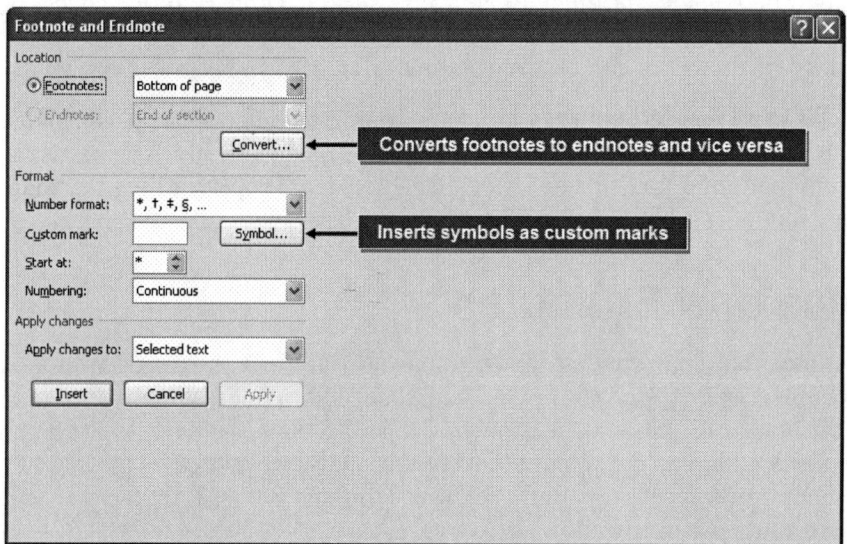

Figure 4-2: Options in the Footnote and Endnote dialog box.

Option	Description
Footnotes or **Endnotes**	Enables you to insert a footnote or an endnote in the document. Selecting either option enables the corresponding drop-down list, where you can select the location of the note.
Convert	Displays the **Convert Notes** dialog box. This dialog box provides you with options that help to convert all footnotes to endnotes, all endnotes to footnotes, or to swap the footnotes and endnotes of the document.
Number format	Provides options that help to format the numbers or symbols that represent the footnote or the endnote. The available formats include asterisks, Roman numerals, and alphabets.
Custom mark	Enables you to insert a custom numbering format for the note type selected. Inserting a custom mark will disable other formatting options.
Symbol	Displays the **Symbol** dialog box. You can choose any symbol to use it as a custom mark.
Start at	Provides options that help to format the number or symbol that represents the first footnote or the endnote in a document.
Numbering	Enables you to specify whether the numbering of the reference notes should be continuous, restart at the end of every section, or restart at the end of every page.
Apply changes to	Enables you to apply the specified format to a specific section or to the whole document.

How to Insert Footnotes and Endnotes

Procedure Reference: Insert a Footnote or an Endnote

To insert a footnote or an endnote:

1. Place the insertion point where you want the note's reference mark to be inserted.
2. Add a note.
   - Use the **Footnote and Endnote** dialog box.
     a. On the **References** tab, in the **Footnotes** group, click the Dialog Box Launcher button.
     b. In the **Footnote and Endnote** dialog box, select **Footnotes** or **Endnotes** and click **Insert.**
   - Use the **Footnotes** group on the **References** tab.
     - Click **Insert Footnote** to insert a footnote.
     - Click **Insert Endnote** to insert an endnote.
   - Or, use shortcut keys.
     - Press Ctrl+Alt+F to insert a footnote.
     - Press Ctrl+Alt+D to insert an endnote.
3. If necessary, select the note and press **Delete** to delete the note.

Procedure Reference: Configure the Footnote and Endnote Formats

To modify a footnote or an endnote:

1. Display the Footnote and Endnote dialog box.
   - On the **References** tab, in the **Footnotes** group, click the Dialog Box Launcher button.
   - Or, right-click the footnote or endnote and choose **Note Options.**
2. Modify the note, as desired.
   - Modify the location of the note.
     - Select **Footnotes**, and from the drop-down list, select **Bottom of page** or **Below text.**
     - Or, select **Endnotes**, and from the drop-down list, select **End of section** or **End of document.**
   - If necessary, convert a note from one type to another.
     a. In the **Location** section, click **Convert.**
     b. In the **Convert Notes** dialog box, select the desired option and click **OK.**
   - Modify the reference mark's format options.
     - From the **Number format** drop-down list, select a number format.
     - In the **Custom mark** text box, enter a symbol.
     - Click **Symbol,** and in the **Symbol** dialog box, select a symbol.
     - In the **Start at** spin box, click the up or down arrow to determine the number or symbol, or type in the spin box.
     - Or, in the **Numbering** drop-down list, determine whether the numbering will be **Continuous, Restart each section,** or **Restart each page.**

3. If necessary, in the **Apply changes to** drop-down list, determine whether to apply changes to either the selected text or to the document as a whole.

4. Click **Insert.**

Manage Footnote and Endnote Locations

You can modify the location of footnotes and endnotes by using the **Footnote and Endnote** dialog box. You can place a footnote either at the bottom of the page or below the text. Endnotes can be placed at the end of a document or section.

Tooltips for Footnotes and Endnotes

You do not have to navigate to the note area to read an endnote or a footnote. Just by placing the insertion point over the note's reference mark, you can view a tooltip containing the note text.

ACTIVITY 4-2
Inserting Footnotes and Endnotes

Before You Begin
1. My Annual Report.docx is open.
2. Turn on the paragraph marks.

Scenario:
While working on the annual report, you have been asked to clarify two points by the lead editor. She wants you to footnote the sources of data used in the chart and table under the Residential section. She has also requested that you add notes explaining why the team was created. To meet company style guidelines, the notes should go at the end of the text's section rather than at the end of the document.

---

1. Insert a footnote explaining the source of the chart and table data.

    a. In the **Navigation** pane, click **Residential.**

    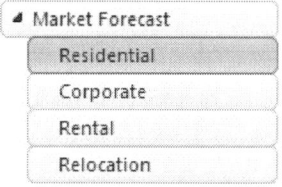

    b. Place the insertion point at the end of the "Residential" paragraph. On the **References** tab, in the **Footnotes** group, click **Insert Footnote.**

    c. Type *The chart and table data are from the Census Bureau's June 2010 New Residential Sales press release.*

---

2. Insert an endnote at the end of the New Relocation Team section.

    a. In the **Navigation** pane, click **New Relocation Team.**

    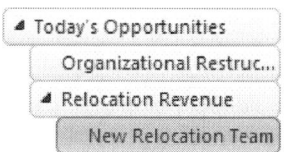

    b. Place the insertion point at the end of the "New Relocation Team" paragraph. In the **Footnotes** group, click the **Footnote & Endnote** dialog box launcher to display the **Footnote and Endnote** dialog box.

    c. In the **Location** section, select **Endnotes.**

    d. From the **Endnotes** drop-down list, select **End of section.**

    e. In the **Format** section, from the **Number format** drop-down list, select **I, II, III.**

f. In the **Apply changes** section, in the **Apply changes to** drop-down list, verify that **This section** is selected and click **Insert.**

g. In the note area, type ***The new team was created to take advantage of current and near-term market trends.***

h. Right-click in the endnote area and choose **Go To Endnote** to navigate to the note's reference mark in the text.

i. Save the document.

TOPIC C
Add Captions

You have inserted footnotes and endnotes in your document. Apart from these references, you may also want to add number and descriptive information to equations, figures, or tables in the document. In this topic, you will add captions.

In textbooks, manuals, and other large documents, objects such as equations, figures, and tables are usually numbered and have a brief description so that they can be easily referred to in the text. You can manually type your own captions, but Word enables you to automatically number captions of equations, figures, or tables without having to manually keep track of the numbering.

Captions

Definition:

A *caption* is a phrase that describes an object, such as a picture, graphic, equation, or table. It identifies the relevance of an object to the content. A caption can be placed above or below the object. In Word, captions can be inserted by using the **Insert Caption** option in the **Captions** group of the **References** tab.

Example:

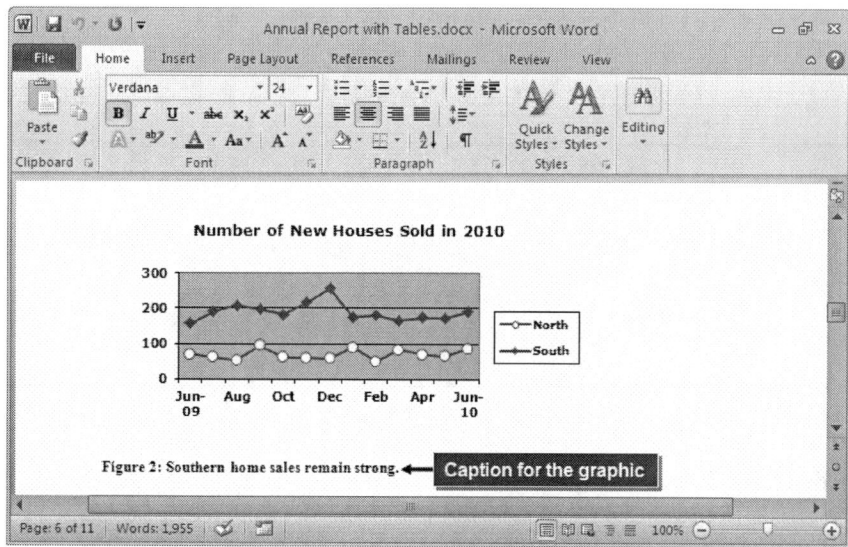

Figure 4-3: An image with caption.

The Caption Dialog Box

The **Caption** dialog box provides options that enable you to add or format a caption.

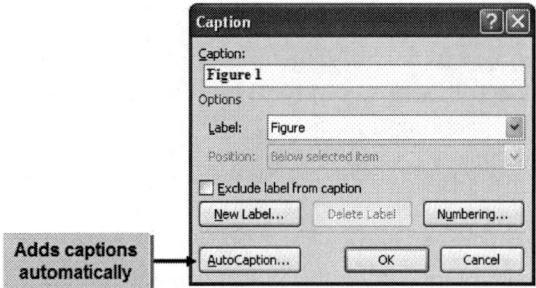

Figure 4-4: *Options available in the Caption dialog box.*

Option	Description
Caption	Enables you to type the caption text. This text box displays the caption title based on the label and numbering format.
Label	Enables you to select the type of caption, such as a table, figure, or equation, to be added to the object.
Position	Enables you to position the caption above or below the selected object.
Exclude label from caption	Removes the label affixed to the caption title.
New Label	Displays the **New Label** dialog box, which enables you to specify a new label.
Delete Label	Enables you to delete a label. This option is active only after a new label is created.
Numbering	Displays the **Caption Numbering** dialog box with options for formatting the numbering of the caption.
AutoCaption	Displays the **AutoCaption** dialog box. This dialog box contains options that enable Word to automatically add captions to objects in a document.

Updating Fields

When you use the **AutoCaption** option, Word may not automatically update all caption numbers. To update all caption numbers and other fields in the document simultaneously, select the entire document and press **F9.** To update the numbering of a single caption, right-click the caption and choose **Update Field.**

How to Add Captions

Procedure Reference: Add a Caption

To add a caption:

1. Browse to the object to which you want to add a caption.

    a. At the bottom of the scroll bar, click the **Select Browse Object** button and choose **Browse by Graphic** to browse by the object you want.

    b. Click either the **Previous** [object] button or the **Next** [object] button to navigate to the last or next instance of the selected object.

2. Display the **Caption** dialog box.

    ● On the **References** tab, in the **Captions** group, click **Insert Caption.**

    ● Or, right-click the selected object and choose **Insert Caption.**

3. In the **Caption** dialog box, in the **Caption** text box, type the description for the object.

4. In the **Options** section, from the **Label** drop-down list, select the type of caption you wish to insert.

5. If necessary, using the options in the **Position** drop-down list, position the caption below or above the object.

6. Click **OK** to insert the caption.

7. If necessary, modify the caption.

    a. Display the **Caption** dialog box.

    b. Specify the desired settings.

    ● Click **New Label**, and in the **New Label** dialog box, type the name of the label and click **OK.**

    ● Click **Numbering**, and in the **Caption Numbering** dialog box, set the format of the caption number and click **OK.**

    c. Click **OK.**

ACTIVITY 4-3
Adding Captions

Before You Begin:
My Annual Report.docx file is open.

Scenario:
You have been asked to create an annual report with supporting objects such as graphics, photographs, and financial charts. You want to make these objects easier to understand and relate to.

1. Add a descriptive figure caption below the Relocation team's organization chart.

    a. Select the organization chart.

    b. On the **References** tab, in the **Captions** group, click **Insert Caption.**

    c. In the **Caption** dialog box, in the **Caption** text box, type *: The Relocation management team.*

    d. In the **Options** section, in the **Label** drop-down list, verify that **Figure** is selected.

    e. In the **Position** drop-down list, verify that **Below selected item** is selected and click **OK.**

2. Add a descriptive figure caption below the house sale and teamwork graphic.

    a. Near the bottom of the scroll bar, click the **Select Browse Object** button and choose **Browse by Graphic**.

    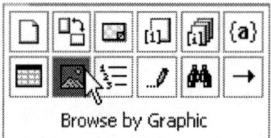
    Browse by Graphic

    b. Click the **Previous Graphic** button twice and select the **Number of New Houses Sold in 2010** chart.

    c. Display the **Caption** dialog box.

    d. In the **Caption** text box, type *: Southern home sales remain strong.*

    e. Verify that, in the **Label** and **Position** drop-down lists, **Figure** and **Below selected item** are selected. Click **OK.**

    f. Similarly, on page 4, add a caption that reads *: Teamwork is critical to our success.* to the teamwork graphic.

3. Add a descriptive table caption below the New Houses Sold table.

a. Click the **Select Browse Object** button and choose **Browse by Table**.

b. Display the **Caption** dialog box.

c. In the **Caption** text box, type *: The North regularly lags behind.*

d. In the **Options** section, from the **Label** drop-down list, select **Table**.

e. From the **Position** drop-down list, select **Below selected item** and click **OK.**

f. Save the document and close it.

TOPIC D
Add Hyperlinks

You have added numbers and descriptive information to illustrations in your document. Now, you may want to provide a means by which users can easily navigate to related content both within and outside of the document. In this topic, you will insert hyperlinks.

There may be times when you want to present detailed reports or long documents to your clients or managers. You can use hyperlinks to enable users to navigate to the desired content rather than providing textual references to the related document. This is a quick way to access related content within and outside a document.

Hyperlinks

Definition:

A *hyperlink* is a navigation tool that links the contents in a document to related information, thereby enabling you to directly navigate to the information. The link is always represented by highlighted words or images. Hyperlinks can be inserted in documents, web pages, text, figures, or tables.

Example:

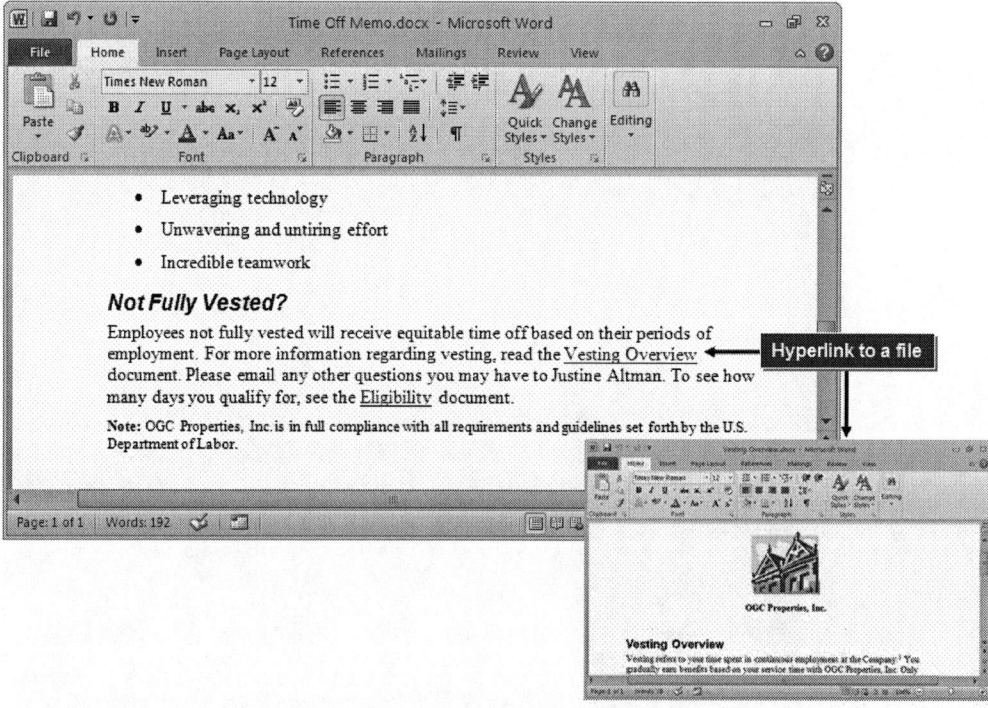

Figure 4-5: A hyperlink text to open another document.

The Insert Hyperlink Dialog Box

The options in the **Insert Hyperlink** dialog box enable you to insert hyperlinks in a new document, an existing document, a web page, or an email address.

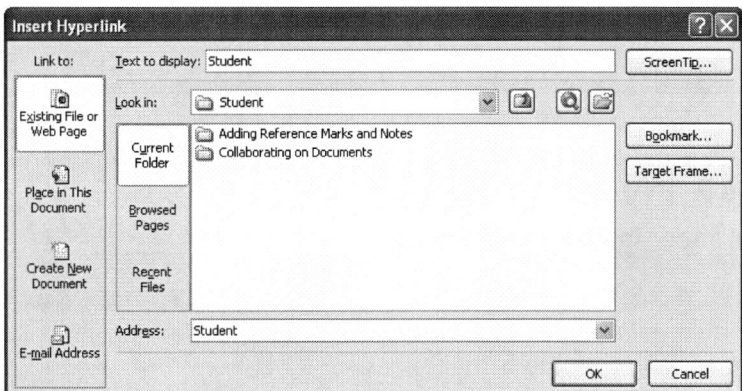

Figure 4-6: *Options in the Insert Hyperlink dialog box*

Section	Description
Link to	Contains options that help to link the current document to an existing file, a web page, content in the same document, a new document, or an email address.
Text to display	Enables you to enter text that is to be displayed as the hyperlink.
Look in	Contains options that help you to navigate to and link a document or web page to the current document. The name and the options in this section vary based on the option selected in the **Link to** section.

 You can insert a ScreenTip that will be displayed when the reader moves the mouse pointer over the hyperlink.

Options in the Look In Section

The section below the **Text to display** section changes based on the option selected in the **Link to** section.

Options in the Link To Section	Description
Existing File or Web Page	Displays the **Look in** section. The various options in this section enable you to link to an already existing document or web page.
Place in This Document	Displays the **Select a place in this document** section. The **Select a place in this document** list box enables you to link to a particular location in the current document.
Create New Document	Displays the **Name of new document** section. The options in this section enable you to link to a new document.

Options in the Link To Section	Description
E-mail Address	Displays the **E-Mail address** section. The options in this section enable you to link to an email address. Clicking the link to the email address displays the **Message** tab in Microsoft® Office Outlook®.

How to Add Hyperlinks

Procedure Reference: Insert a Hyperlink

To insert a hyperlink to a document:

1. Place the insertion point where you wish to insert the hyperlink or select the text or graphic you want to use as a hyperlink.

2. Display the **Insert Hyperlink** dialog box.

    *   On the **Insert** tab, in the **Links** group, click **Hyperlink.**

    *   Press Ctrl+K.

    *   Or, right-click the selected text and choose **Hyperlink.**

3. In the **Text to display** text box, type the text that is to be displayed as the hyperlink. If you have selected the text, it is displayed by default and can be modified, if desired.

4. If necessary, add a ScreenTip.

    a. Click **ScreenTip**.

    b. In the **Set Hyperlink Screen Tip** dialog box, type the screen tip that you want to display and click **OK.**

5. In the **Link to** section, select the desired option.

    *   Link the document to an existing file or a web page.

        a. Select **Existing File or Web Page.**

        b. In the **Look in** section, select the file to be linked to and click **OK** to link the file.

    *   Link the document to a location within the document.

        a. Select **Place in This Document.**

        b. In the **Select a place in this document** section, select a desired location in the document and click **OK** to link to selected location within the document.

    *   Link the document to a new document.

        a. Select **Create New Document.**

        b. In the **Name of new document** text box, type a name of your choice to name the document.

        c. In the **Full path** section, click **Change** and select a file path to store the document.

        d. In the **When to edit** section, select an option to edit the document and click **OK** to create a link to the new document.

    *   Link the document to Microsoft Outlook message window.

        a. Select **E-mail Address.**

    b.   In the **E-mail address** text box, type the e-mail address you want to link to.

    c.   In the **Subject** text box, type the text you want to appear as the subject and click **OK** to link the email address to your document.

6.   If necessary, Ctrl-click or right-click the hyperlink and choose **Open Hyperlink** to navigate to the linked text or content.

7.   If necessary, right-click the hyperlink, choose **Edit Hyperlink**, make the necessary changes, and click **OK** to modify the hyperlink.

8.   If necessary, delete a hyperlink.

-    Delete the hyperlink using the **Edit Hyperlink** dialog box.

    a.   Right-click the link and choose **Edit Hyperlink.**

    b.   In the **Edit Hyperlink** dialog box, click **Remove Link.**

-    Or, select the hyperlink and press **Delete.**

Procedure Reference: Use a Hyperlink as a Bookmark

To use a hyperlink as a bookmark:

1.   Place the insertion point where you wish to insert the hyperlink or select the text or graphic you want to use as a hyperlink.

2.   Display the **Insert Hyperlink** dialog box.

3.   In the **Insert Hyperlink** dialog box, in the **Address** text-box, type the destination location for the hyperlink.

4.   Click **Bookmark**, and in the **Select Place in Document** dialog box, in the **Select an existing place in the document** section, select a location and click **OK.**

5.   In the **Insert Hyperlink** dialog box, click **OK.**

The Edit Hyperlink Dialog Box

The **Edit Hyperlink** dialog box contains options that help you to modify or edit a hyperlink. The options in the **Edit Hyperlink** dialog box are similar to the options in the **Insert Hyperlink** dialog box. However, this dialog box provides an additional option for deleting selected links.

ACTIVITY 4-4
Inserting Hyperlinks

Data Files:

C:\084584Data\Adding Reference Marks and Notes\Time Off Memo.docx, C:\084584Data\Adding Reference Marks and Notes\Eligibility.docx, C:\084584Data\Adding Reference Marks and Notes\Vesting Overview.docx

Scenario:

As an HR executive, you have been assigned the task of composing a memo to inform employees about the number of days off they are allowed. Right now, details pertaining to the different types of employee time-offs are available in different documents. You need to include all the information in these documents in your memo without making it look cluttered.

---

1. Link the Time Off Memo.docx file to the Vesting Overview.docx file.

   a. From the C:\084584Data\Adding Reference Marks and Notes folder, open the Time Off Memo.docx file.

   b. Scroll down, and in the **Not Fully Vested** paragraph, in the second line, select the text "Vesting Overview."

   c. On the **Insert** tab, in the **Links** group, click **Hyperlink.**

   d. In the **Insert Hyperlink** dialog box, click **ScreenTip.**

   e. In the **Set Hyperlink ScreenTip** dialog box, in the **ScreenTip text** text box, type ***Click here to display the Vesting Overview.docx file.*** and click **OK.**

   f. In the **Link to** section, verify that **Existing File or Web Page** is selected.

   g. In the **Look in** list box, select **Vesting Overview.docx** and click **OK.**

   h. Notice that the hyperlink is highlighted in blue. Place the mouse pointer over the Vesting Overview hyperlink to view the screen tip.

   i. Ctrl-click the hyperlink to open the Vesting Overview.docx file.

   j. Close the Vesting Overview.docx file.

---

2. Link the word "Eligibility" to the Eligibility.docx file.

   a. In the first paragraph below the title "Not Fully Vested?" right-click the word "Eligibility" in the last line and choose **Hyperlink.**

   b. Insert a screen tip that reads ***Click here to display the Eligibility document.***

   c. In the **Look in** section, select **Eligibility.docx** and click **OK.**

   d. Notice that the hyperlink is highlighted in blue to distinguish it from the rest of the text. Save the document as ***My Time Off Memo*** and close it.

TOPIC E

Add Cross-References

You created links to specific contents to add clarity to your document without repeating information. Similarly, bringing in references to a particular page or text in a document enables the reader to refer to that content in case of doubt. In this topic, you will add cross-references within your document.

You may want to present reports with more details but with a minimum page count. You may want to refer to certain charts and tables to add clarity to the text, but adding the charts and tables to the document would again increase the page count. By using cross-references, you can add clarity to the text while still maintaining your desired page count.

Cross-References

Definition:

A *cross-reference* directs the reader to a particular location in a document. It always indicates the related contents to the reader. Cross-references may refer to text, graphics, tables, or pictures in a document, and can be added as hyperlinks.

Example:

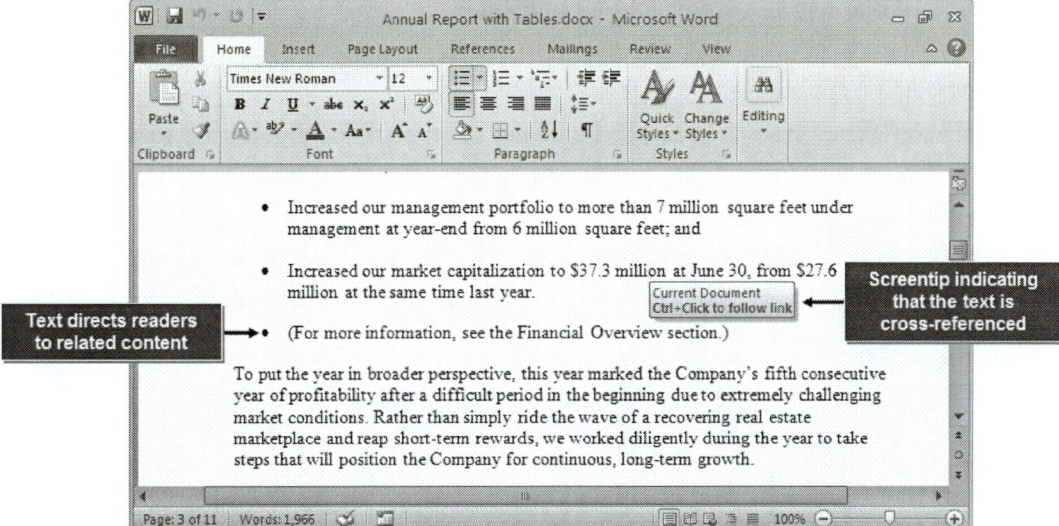

Figure 4-7: A cross-reference in a document.

The Cross-Reference Dialog Box

The **Cross-reference** dialog box contains options to insert a cross-reference to text or other objects in a document.

Option	Description
Reference type	Displays a list of items you may want to reference.
Insert reference to	Displays a list of items you may want to insert in the cross-reference. The options displayed depend upon the reference type selected.
Insert as hyperlink	Enables you to add the cross-reference as a hyperlink that directs the user to the location specified in the cross-reference.
For which [Object]	Displays the list of items available in the document for the selected reference type.

How to Add Cross-References

Procedure Reference: Insert and Update Cross-References

To insert and update cross-references:

1. Place the insertion point at the location where you want to insert the cross-reference.
2. Type the text that will precede the cross-reference.
3. On the **Insert** tab, in the **Links** group, click **Cross-reference** to display the **Cross-reference** dialog box.
4. From the **Reference type** drop-down list, select the type of item you want to reference.
5. From the **Insert reference to** drop-down list, select the type of item you want to insert in the document.
6. If necessary, check **Insert as hyperlink.**
7. In the **For which** [Object] list box, select the specific item the cross-reference needs to refer to.

 Some reference types, such as figures, require a caption for them to be displayed in the **For which** list box.

8. Click **Insert** to place the cross-reference.
9. Click **Close** to close the **Cross-reference** dialog box.
10. If necessary, finish typing the remaining text supporting the cross-reference.
11. If necessary, Ctrl-click the cross-reference to navigate to the cross-referenced location.
12. If necessary, update the cross-reference.
    - Right-click the cross-reference and choose **Update Field** to update the current cross-reference.
    - Or, select the entire document and press F9 to update all the fields in the document.

Shaded Cross-References

You can make cross-references and other fields appear shaded all the time. To do so, in the **Advanced** category of the **Word Options** dialog box, in the **Show document content** section, from the **Field shading** drop-down list, select **Always.**

Go back (Shift F-5)

ACTIVITY 4-5
Inserting Cross-References

Data Files:

C:\084584Data\Adding Reference Marks and Notes\Annual Report with Tables.docx

Scenario:

In order to direct the reader's attention to headings, figures, and tables in the stockholder report, you type text references, such as "See Figure 1," in the report. However, you realize that if the document text changes, the references may no longer be accurate.

---

1. Cross-reference the "Financial Overview" heading in the last bullet point below the "Fiscal Accomplishments" title.

   a. From the C:\084584Data\Adding Reference Marks and Notes folder, open the Annual Report with Tables.docx file.

   b. Display the **Advanced** category in the **Word Options** dialog box.

   c. Scroll down and in the **Show document content** section, from the **Field shading** drop-down list, select **Always** and click **OK**.

   d. Display the **Bookmark** dialog box.

   e. Navigate to **Fiscal** and close the dialog box.

   f. Place the insertion point at the end of the last bullet point and press **Enter**.

   g. Type *(For more information, see the* and press the **Spacebar**.

   h. On the **Insert** tab, in the **Links** group, click **Cross-reference**.

   i. In the **Cross-reference** dialog box, from the **Reference type** drop-down list, select **Heading.**

   j. In the **Insert reference to** drop-down list, verify that **Heading Text** is selected.

   k. In the **For which heading** list box, select **Financial Overview** and click **Insert**.

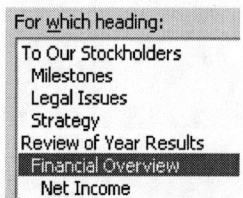

   l. Click **Close** to close the **Cross-reference** dialog box.

   m. Press the **Spacebar** and type *section.)* to complete the supporting text after the **Financial Overview** cross-reference.

   n. Ctrl-click the "Financial Overview" link to display the **Financial Overview** section.

---

2. Cross-reference Figure 1.

   a. In the **Navigation** pane, click **Strategy.**

   b. In the third line of the paragraph, place the insertion point before the sentence that begins with "More than providing."

   c. Type *(See* and press the **Spacebar.**

   d. Display the **Cross-reference** dialog box.

   e. From the **Reference type** drop-down list, select **Figure.**

   f. From the **Insert reference to** drop-down list, select **Only label and number.**

   g. In the **For which caption** list box, verify that **Figure 1: Teamwork is critical to our success** is selected.

   h. Click **Insert** and close the **Cross-reference** dialog box.

   i. Type **)** and press the **Spacebar** to complete the supporting text after the cross-reference.

3. Cross-reference Table 1.

   a. In the **Navigation** pane, click **Residential.**

   b. In the third line of the paragraph, place the insertion point before the sentence that begins with "This ongoing trend... "

   c. Type *(See the data in* and press the **Spacebar.**

   d. Display the **Cross-reference** dialog box.

   e. From the **Reference type** drop-down list, select **Table.**

   f. From the **Insert reference to** drop-down list, select **Only label and number.**

   g. In the **For which caption** list box, verify that **Table 1: The North regularly lags behind** is selected.

   h. Click **Insert** and close the **Cross-reference** dialog box.

   i. After the Table 1 cross-reference, type *.)* and press the **Spacebar** to complete the supporting text.

   j. Save the document as *My Annual Report with Tables* and close it.

TOPIC F
Add Citations and a Bibliography

You know how to provide cross-references for content that is in another part of a document. In the course of your work, you may have referred to various materials when creating a document. The credibility of your document is, therefore, dependent on the references that you provide. In this topic, you will add citations and a bibliography.

Just as the validity of a news story is dependent on its sources, the relevance of a content is dependent on its references. Therefore, it becomes necessary for you to give your readers credible references. Word simplifies this process by enabling you to enter citations throughout a document, which will allow for the creation of a bibliography using a single command.

Sources

A *source* is a reference material from which content is borrowed. For instance, text, graphics, pictures, tables, or an entire content can be used as reference materials.

Citations

A *citation* is a reference to any legal source of content. You can use the **Insert Citation** command to create a citation. Citations can be made in the body of text or in footnotes found at the bottom of a page.

Bibliographies

A *bibliography* is a list of references usually inserted at the end of a section or document. Bibliographic content helps to identify the edition, date of issue, authorship, and typography of books or other written material.

Bibliography Citation Styles

Bibliography citation styles provide a consistent appearance to the reference information in a document. Word provides users with numerous built-in reference styles.

Style	Description
APA Fifth Edition	The **APA Fifth Edition** or American Psychological Association style is usually used as a reference style in psychological, educational, and other social sciences-based documents.
Chicago Fifteenth Edition	The **Chicago Fifteenth Edition** style is usually used in noneducational documents such as magazines and newspapers.
GB7714 2005	**GB7714 2005** is a style type followed by the Standardization Administration of China.
GOST – Name Sort	**GOST – Name Sort** is a style type followed by The Federal Agency of the Russian Federation on Technical Regulating and Metrology.
GOST – Title Sort	**GOST – Title Sort** is a style type followed by The Federal Agency of the Russian Federation on Technical Regulating and Metrology.

Style	Description
ISO 690 – First Element and Date	**ISO 690 – First Element and Date** is a style type followed by the International Organization for Standardization.
ISO 690 – Numerical Reference	**ISO 690 – Numerical Reference** is a style type followed by the International Organization for Standardization.
MLA Sixth Edition	The **MLA Sixth Edition** or Modern Language Association style is used in documents related to literature, arts, and humanities.
SIST02	**SIST02** is also called the Standards for Information of Science and Technology style. This style is used mostly in Asian countries.
Turabian Sixth Edition	**Turabian Sixth Edition** style is used by students for their academic documents.

How to Add Citations and a Bibliography

Procedure Reference: Insert a Citation

To insert a citation:

1. Place the insertion point at the location where you want to insert the citation.

2. On the **References** tab, in the **Citations & Bibliography** group, from the **Style** drop-down list, select a style.

3. Click **Insert Citation** and choose an appropriate option.

   - Choose **Add New Source**, and in the **Create Source** dialog box, specify the options in order to add the information.

     a. From the **Type of Source** drop-down list, select the appropriate source.

     b. Based on the type of source, fill in the bibliography fields.

     c. If necessary, check **Show All Bibliography Fields**.

     d. Click **OK** to close the dialog box.

   - Or, choose **Add New Placeholder**, and in the **Placeholder Name** dialog box, type a name for the placeholder and click **OK** to add a placeholder to fill in the information later.

The Create Source Dialog Box

The **Create Source** dialog box contains options that enable you to create a new source for citations and bibliographies. The options available for creating a source vary depending on the reference style selected.

Option	Description
Type of Source	Displays a list of source types from which the content has been borrowed.
Bibliography Fields	Enables users to enter information about the source.
Show All Bibliography Fields	Displays all the fields related to the reference style and source selected.
Tag name	Identifies a particular source.

Procedure Reference: Add a Bibliography

To add a bibliography:

1. Click at the end of the document.
2. On the **References** tab, in the **Citations & Bibliography** group, click the **Bibliography** drop-down and choose **Insert Bibliography**, or, in the **Built-In** section, choose **Bibliography.**

 To insert a bibliography, you must already have inserted a source using the **Create Source** dialog box.

Procedure Reference: Modify a Source

To modify a source:

1. Place the mouse pointer over the citation source or placeholder to display the field.
2. Right-click the citation, source, or placeholder, and choose **Edit Source.**
3. In the **Edit Source** dialog box, add or modify the details and click **OK.**

The Edit Source Dialog Box

Whenever you wish to modify the information about a source, you can display the **Edit Source** dialog box. The options in the **Edit Source** dialog box are similar to the options in the **Create Source** dialog box.

Procedure Reference: Modify a Citation

To modify a citation:

1. Place the mouse pointer over the citation source or placeholder to display its field.
2. Right-click the citation and choose **Edit Citation.**
3. In the **Edit Citation** dialog box, set the options.

   - In the **Add** section, in the **Pages** text box, type the pages that you wish to include as part of the citation.

   - In the **Suppress** section, check the check box to prevent the author, year, or title information from being displayed.

4. Click **OK.**

The Edit Citation Dialog Box

You can use the **Edit Citation** dialog box to include the pages you want to refer to along with the citation. In addition, you can prevent the author, year, and title information from being displayed in the document.

Procedure Reference: Modify a Bibliography

To modify a bibliography:

1. On the **References** tab, in the **Citations & Bibliography** group, click **Manage Sources.**
2. In the **Source Manager** dialog box, in the **Sources available in** section, in the **Current List** list box, select the source and click **Edit.**
3. In the **Edit Source** dialog box, modify the details.
4. Click **OK** to close the **Edit Source** dialog box.

5. Click **Close** to close the **Source Manager** dialog box.

6. Press F9 to update the bibliography field.

The Source Manager Dialog Box

The **Source Manager** dialog box is used to filter the source that is to be added, as a bibliographic reference, from the various sources added to the document. Using the options in the **Search** section, you can search for a specific source type based on the author, tag, title, or year information.

The **Sources available in** section displays the list of sources available in the master and current documents. Using the options here, you can also copy source content from the **Master List** to the **Current List**, delete any particular source, edit source information, or create a new source. The **Preview** section displays the style in which the source will be displayed, both as a citation and a bibliography.

ACTIVITY 4-6
Adding Citations and a Bibliography

Data Files:

C:\084584Data\Adding Reference Marks and Notes\Financial Report.docx

Scenario:

You have compiled the financial report for your company's online journal by procuring information from the finance and administrative departments. You want to acknowledge these sources of information in your document to ensure that there are no legal issues with your document. In instances where you are not sure of the department you obtained the information, you decide to include placeholders.

1. Designate Samantha Smith as a source.

   a. From the C:\084584Data\Adding Reference Marks and Notes folder, open the Financial Report.docx file.

   b. Navigate to the title "Economic Indicators on the Web."

   c. In the first line, click after the text "The Economic Indicators Web site."

   d. On the **References** tab, in the **Citations & Bibliography** group, from the **Style** drop-down list, select **Chicago Fifteenth Edition.**

   e. Click the **Insert Citation** drop-down and choose **Add New Source.**

   f. In the **Create Source** dialog box, from the **Type of Source** drop-down list, select **Report.**

   g. In the **Author** text box, type *Samantha Smith*

   h. In the **Title** text box, type *Economics Review 2008*

   i. In the **Year** text box, type *June, 2008* and click **OK.**

   j. Notice that **(Smith June, 2008)** appears beside the text "The Economic Indicators Web site," indicating the addition of the citation.

   ·(Smith·June,2008)·

2. Insert a placeholder to mark the "Net Income" citation.

   a. Navigate to the title "Net Income."

   b. Place the insertion point at the end of the first paragraph.

   c. In the **Citations & Bibliography** group, click the **Insert Citation** drop-down and choose **Add New Placeholder.**

    d.   In the **Placeholder Name** dialog box, verify that the name of the placeholder is indicated as **Placeholder1** and click **OK.**

·(Placeholder1)¶

3.   Designate Mike Nash as a source.

    a.   Navigate to the end of the document and place the insertion point before the last paragraph mark.

    b.   Display the **Create Source** dialog box.

    c.   From the **Type of Source** drop-down list, scroll down and select **Web site.**

    d.   In the **Author** text box, type *Mike Nash*

    e.   In the **Name of Web Page** text box, type *Economic Indicators*

    f.   In the **URL** text box, type *www.economicindicators.example* and click **OK.**

4.   Insert a bibliography.

    a.   Verify that the insertion point is at the end of the document and press **Enter.**

    b.   On the **References** tab, in the **Citations & Bibliography** group, click the **Bibliography** drop-down and choose **Bibliography.**

    c.   Notice that the bibliography is added at the end of the document.

·**Bibliography**¶

Nash,·Mike.·*Economic·Indicators*.·n.d.·www.economicindicators.example.¶
Smith,·Samantha.·"Economics·Review·2008."·June,·2008.¶
  ¶

    d.   Save the document as *My Financial Report*

ACTIVITY 4-7
Modifying the Citations and Bibliography

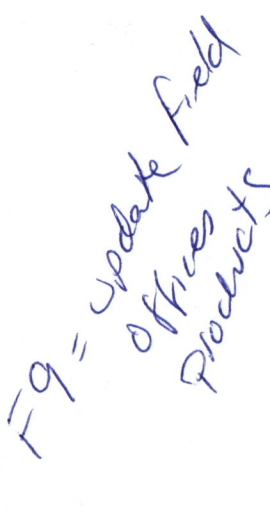

Before You Begin:

My Financial Report.docx is open.

Scenario:

You just received the financial report from your editor. She has pointed out a few issues that need to be updated in the document before returning it to her. She has asked you to cite the year in which the content was updated on the website. Apart from this, she has suggested that including the author name for the economic review is not necessary. Also, you need to update the placeholder so that she can include the report in the journal.

---

1. Update the placeholder.

    a. Navigate to **Net Income.**

    b. Under the title "Net Income," right-click **Placeholder1** and choose **Edit Source.**

    c. In the **Edit Source** dialog box, in the **Type of Source** drop-down list, scroll up and select **Book.**

    d. In the **Author** text box, type *Ashton, Chris*

    e. In the **Year** text box, type *Jan, 2009* and click **OK.**

    f. Notice that Placeholder1 is now updated.

    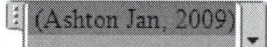

---

2. Hide the author information.

    a. Navigate to "Economic Indicators on the Web."

    b. In the first line of the paragraph, right-click the citation and choose **Edit Citation.**

    c. In the **Edit Citation** dialog box, in the **Suppress** section, check **Author** and click **OK** to close the **Edit Citation** dialog box.

---

3. Update the bibliography information for Mike Nash.

    a. On the **References** tab, in the **Citations & Bibliography** group, click **Manage Sources.**

    b. In the **Source Manager** dialog box, in the **Sources available in** section, in the **Current List** list box, select **Nash, Mike; Economic Indicators** and click **Edit.**

    c. In the **Edit Source** dialog box, in the **Year** text box, type *Feb, 2009* and click **OK.**

    d. In the **Microsoft Word** warning message box, click **Yes.**

---

e.   Click **Close** to close the **Source Manager** dialog box.

4.   Update the references.

a.   Scroll down to the end of the document and click anywhere in the document.

b.   Select the entire document.

c.   Press **F9** to update the references.

d.   Observe that the bibliography has been updated.

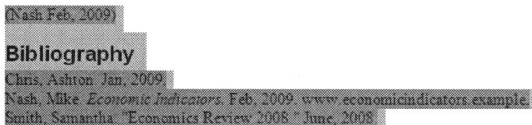

e.   Close the **Navigation** pane.

f.   Save the document and close it.

Lesson 4 Follow-up

In this lesson, you added descriptive reference marks. Footnotes, endnotes, citations, and bibliographies supply the reader with detailed explanations and source information, while bookmarks and hyperlinks enable them to navigate quickly and easily to marked locations. Captions and cross-references aid in increased understanding of the content.

1. **Considering the types of documents you create, how might you use reference marks and notes to make information more accessible to readers?**

2. **Of the different types of reference marks and notes, which ones are you most likely to use in your documents?**

5 | Simplifying the Use of Long Documents

Lesson Time: 1 hour(s), 30 minutes

Lesson Objectives:

In this lesson, you will simplify the use of long documents.

You will:

● Insert blank and cover pages.

● Insert an index.

● Insert a table of figures.

● Insert a table of authorities.

● Insert a table of contents.

● Create a master document.

Introduction

You added source information using reference marks and notes. To help readers locate figures, tables, graphics, or content in a document, you have to include tables listing all relevant items or keywords with their page numbers. In this lesson, you will insert reference lists in documents.

Locating information in long printed documents is difficult if you are not sure of the location of keywords. Reference tables listing important objects, terms, and graphics along with their location can be handy. The advanced features in Word let you make short work of inserting reference tables in any type of document.

TOPIC A
Insert Blank and Cover Pages

You added reference marks and notes to your document to aid readers' in their understanding of the contents and to navigate quickly and easily. Adding cover and blank pages provides you with a simple way to break the monotony in long documents. In this topic, you will insert blank and cover pages.

When you walk into a store, the first thing that attracts you to a product is its packaging. Likewise, a nicely designed cover page is the finishing touch that will make any document to stand out. Word offers a range of built-in options that can help you create and format your cover pages with ease. Plus, Word enables you to insert blank pages at will, which also help readability by breaking up large blocks of text and visually differentiating major sections.

Cover and Blank Pages

Many documents have an attractive first page that includes information such as the title, subtitle, author's name, and date. The **Cover Page** drop-down, which displays a gallery of various built-in cover pages, enables you to choose from various styles. Each cover page style includes standard fields for customizing text. The cover page you select will be inserted at the beginning of a document, before the first page. You can also insert blank pages in your document to break the monotony of content and differentiate major sections. Blank pages are usually used for indicating section breaks and are, therefore, inserted between sections and at the end of a document.

How to Insert Blank and Cover Pages

Procedure Reference: Insert Blank or Cover Pages

To insert blank or cover pages:

1. Place the insertion point at the appropriate location.

   ● Place the insertion point at the beginning of the document to insert a cover page.

   ● Or, place the insertion point before or after the text or page where you want to insert the blank page.

2. Insert a page using the **Pages** group on the **Insert** tab.

   ● From the **Cover Page** gallery, select the desired style and type the desired content to create a cover page.

   ● Click **Blank Page** to insert a blank page.

    When you try to insert a blank page before a section break, Word inserts a page break before the section break.

3. If you inserted a cover page, update the content of the fields in the page with your specific text.

ACTIVITY 5-1
Inserting Blank and Cover Pages

Data Files:

C:\084584Data\Simplifying the Use of Long Documents\Annual Report With Tables.docx

Scenario:

The financial report for the year is updated and ready for printing. However, in the print preview, the document seems to have an abrupt starting without any kind of introduction. You decide to add a cover and a blank page to the report to make it look professionally designed, give a suitable title, and add a blank page after the index.

---

1. Insert a cover page.

    a.   From the C:\084584Data\Simplifying the Use of Long Documents folder, open the Annual Report With Tables.docx file.

    b.   Verify that the mouse pointer is placed at the beginning of the document.

    c.   On the **Insert** tab, in the **Pages** group, click the **Cover Page** drop-down to display the cover pages gallery.

    d.   In the gallery, scroll down and select **Cubicles.**

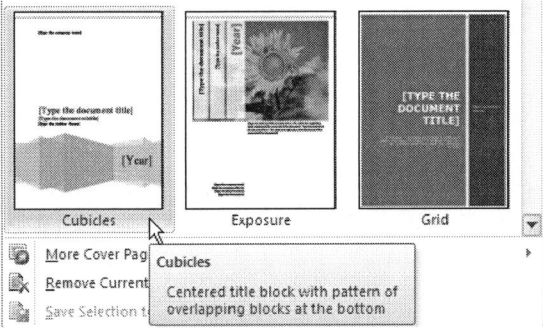

---

2. Update the information in the cover page.

    a.   Click the text **"[Type the company name]"** and type *OGC Properties*

    b.   Scroll down, click the text **"[Type the document title]"** and type *OGC Properties Inc., Annual Report*

    c.   Click the text **"[Type the document subtitle]"** and type *Annual Report*

    d.   Select the user name below the text "Annual Report" and type your name.

---

e.   Click the text **"[Year]"** and, from the date field placeholder drop-down list, select **Today.**

3.   Insert a blank page and preview the document.

a.   Scroll down and place the insertion point before the heading "OGC Properties, Inc."

b.   On the **Insert** tab, in the **Pages** group, click **Blank Page** to insert a blank page.

c.   On the **View** tab, in the **Zoom** group, click **Two Pages** to preview the document.

d.   Scroll up to view the cover and blank page inserted in the report.

e.   Save the file as *My Annual Report with Tables*

TOPIC B

Insert an Index

In the previous topic, you inserted a cover page and a blank page. Now, in order to complete the document, you want to provide a detailed listing of the important sections in the document along with their page numbers so that people can refer to the listing to locate information. In this topic, you will insert an index.

Providing an index gives readers a way to locate marked entries wherever they appear in a document. When you use Word to insert an index, the index is automatically updated whenever a document's text or pagination changes.

The Index Dialog Box

The **Index** dialog box enables you to insert, format, and modify the index in a document.

Option	Enables You To
Print Preview	Preview the index as it would appear in a printed Word document.
Type	Determine the manner in which the text in the index is to be displayed. The text can be either listed or run-in as continuous entries.
Columns	Select and insert the desired number of columns the index will contain.
Language	Set the desired language for the index entry.
Right align page numbers	Align the page numbers in the index toward the right margin of the document.
Tab leader	Set the desired tab leader.
Formats	Format the index.
Mark Entry	Access the **Mark Index Entry** dialog box, which enables you to locate and mark text in a document as index entries.
AutoMark	Mark new entries for the index automatically.
Modify	Access the **Style** dialog box that has options for formatting the text entries in the index.

In the **Index** dialog box, the **Indented** option, selected by default, lists the marked content based on hierarchy. If you select **Run-in,** the content will be displayed as continuous text with one entry following the other on the same line.

The Mark Index Entry Dialog Box

The **Mark Index Entry** dialog box contains options to locate and mark text in a document as index entries.

Section	Enables You To
Index	Specify the main index entry text and subentries.
Options	Specify the type of index entry.
Page number format	Select a format for the page numbers that will appear in the index.

Mark Index Entries Options

By default, index entries use the **Current page** option to identify the marked term or phrase on a particular page. The **Cross-reference** option allows you to redirect the reader to another term in the index. The **Page range** option allows you to type or select a bookmark from the **Bookmark** drop-down list. For example, if the reader looks up the word "Colonial" in the index, you can use the **Cross-Reference** option to insert "See Housing Types" to redirect the reader to the "Housing Types" index entry.

Subentries

An index usually contains a main entry and one or more subentries. The main entries could be the headings in a document, whereas subentries are other information in the document that you may want to read about in relation to the main entry.

The Concordance File

A *concordance file* is a document with a two-column table used for marking index entries automatically in another document. The first column lists the terms and phrases you want marked as index entries. These terms and phrases should be entered exactly as they appear in the document. The second column contains the actual index entries for the text in the first column.

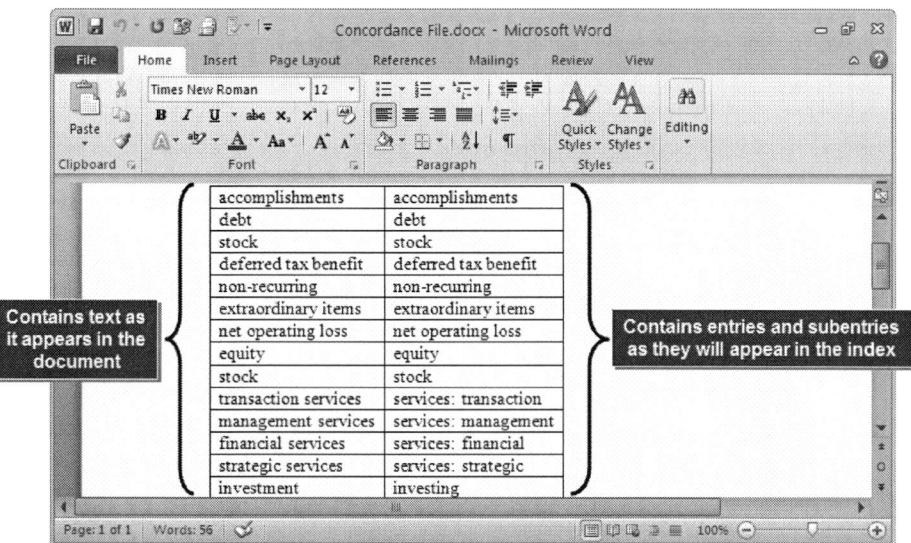

Figure 5-1: *A concordance file with index entries.*

The Open Index AutoMark File Dialog Box

The **Open Index AutoMark File** dialog box enables you to navigate to the concordance file. Opening the concordance file automatically marks the text in the concordance file as entries for the index in the current document.

The Style Dialog Box

The **Style** dialog box contains various options to format the index style.

Option	Description
Styles	Displays a list of default index styles available in the document.
Preview	Displays a preview of the selected style.
Modify	Displays the **Modify Style** dialog box with options for modifying the selected index style.

The Modify Style Dialog Box

The **Modify Style** dialog box contains additional options to format an index.

Option	Enables You To
Properties	View the name of the selected index style, type of style, origin format, and the style followed in the paragraph following an index entry.
Formatting	Format an index entry by specifying the font, font size, font styles, and font color.
Alignment	Format the text alignment, spacing, and indentation of an index entry.
Preview	Preview the formatting set for an index entry.
Add to Quick Style list	Add the currently set format as a style in the **Quick Style** list.
Automatically update	Automatically update the formatting style of the entries in other indices as well.
Only in this document	Specify the formatting options for the current document only.
New documents based on this template	Set the current format of index entries as a template for use in other documents.

How to Insert an Index

Procedure Reference: Mark Text for Indexing

To mark text for indexing:

1. Mark text.

    ● Mark text manually.

    a. Select the text that you want to mark as an index entry.

    b. On the **References** tab, in the **Index** group, click **Mark Entry** to display the **Mark Index Entry** dialog box.

     You can also press **Alt+Shift+X** to display the **Mark Index Entry** dialog box.

    c. Specify the desired options in the **Mark Index Entry** dialog box.

    ■ In the **Main entry** text box, type or edit the content of the entry.

    ■ In the **Subentry** text box, type the subentry to the main index entry.

    ■ In the **Options** section, set the type of index entry for the selected text.

    ■ In the **Page number format** section, check **Bold** or **Italic** to select a format for the page numbers that will appear in the index.

    ■ Click **Mark** to mark that specific entry.

    ■ Click **Mark All** to mark similar entries in the document.

- Click **Close** to close the **Mark Index Entry** dialog box.
- Mark text automatically by using a concordance file.
  a. On the **References** tab, in the **Index** group, click **Insert Index.**
  b. In the **Index** dialog box, click **AutoMark.**
  c. In the **Open Index AutoMark File** dialog box, navigate to and select the concordance file and click **Open.**
2. If necessary, modify the document.
  a. If necessary, display the formatting marks and the **Navigation** pane.
  b. Navigate to the index entry you wish to modify.
  c. In the entry's field code, edit any text within the quotation marks.
3. If necessary, delete an index entry.
  a. If necessary, display the formatting marks.
  b. Scroll down to the desired index entry field code, select it, and press **Delete.**

Index Entry Field Codes

When you mark an index entry, the entry is represented by a field code that is displayed when the formatting mark option is enabled. The field code displays the index entry within quotes and the term "XE" precedes the index entry. To edit the index entry without making changes to the contents, you need to change the text within the quotes in the field code.

Procedure Reference: Create a Concordance File

To create a concordance file:

1. Open a new document and insert a two column table.
2. In the left column, enter the first word or phrase that you want marked as index entries.
3. In the right column, enter the actual index entries for the text in the first column.
4. Save and close the document.

Procedure Reference: Insert an Index

To insert an index:

1. Place the insertion point where you want to insert the index.
2. On the **References** tab, in the **Index** group, click **Insert Index.**
3. In the **Index** dialog box, on the **Index** tab, set the desired options.
   - In the **Type** section, specify the index type.
     - Select **Indented** to display each index entry in a new line.
     - Select **Run-in** to display index entries continuously.
   - In the **Columns** spin box, set the number of columns for the index.
   - From the **Language** drop-down list, select the language you want to apply to the index.
4. If necessary, mark an entry for the index.
   - Click **Mark Entry** to display the **Mark Index Entry** dialog box and manually mark more entries for the index.
   - Or, click **AutoMark** to automatically mark index entries.

5. If necessary, click **Modify** to display the **Style** dialog box and modify the formatting of the index.

    a. In the **Style** dialog box, select the desired index style and click **Modify.**

    b. In the **Modify Style** dialog box, set the desired formatting options.

    c. Click **OK** to close the **Modify Style** dialog box.

    d. Click **OK** to close the **Style** dialog box.

6. Click **OK** to insert the index.

7. If necessary, update the index.

    a. Locate the index you wish to update.

    b. Update the index.

       ● Right-click the index and choose **Update Field.**

       ● Select the index entries and press **F9.**

       ● Or, on the **References** tab, in the **Index** group, click **Update Index.**

ACTIVITY 5-2
Indexing a Document

Data Files:

C:\084584Data\Simplifying the Use of Long Documents\Concordance File.docx

Before You Begin:

1. My Annual Report With Tables.docx is open.

2. Display the **Navigation** pane.

3. On the **View** tab, in the **Zoom** group, click **100%.**

Scenario:

With the annual report now complete, you have to add the index and format it according to your company's output standards. To make indexing an easy step, you have created a concordance file containing some of the most common terms used in business documents.

---

1. Display the **Mark Index Entry** dialog box.

   a. Using the **Navigation** pane, navigate to the "Milestones" heading.

   b. In the second line of the paragraph below the "Milestones" heading, select the word **"commercial."**

   c. On the **References** tab, in the **Index** group, click **Mark Entry.**

---

2. Mark all instances of the word "commercial," so that it appears as a subentry for "Services."

   a. In the **Mark Index Entry** dialog box, in the **Main entry** text box, type *Services* and press **Tab.**

   b. In the **Subentry** text box, type *commercial*

   c. In the **Options** section, verify that **Current page** is selected.

   d. Click **Mark All** and click **Close.**

---

3. Enable AutoMark for the rest of the document using the concordance file.

   a. On the **References** tab, in the **Index** group, click **Insert Index.**

   b. In the **Index** dialog box, click **AutoMark.**

   c. In the **Open Index AutoMark File** dialog box, navigate to the C:\084584Data\ Simplifying the Use of Long Documents folder and open the Concordance File document.

---

d. Observe that the terms "accomplishments," "non-recurring," "debt," and "equity" are marked as index entries.

> Among our fiscal accomplishment§·XE·"accomplishments"·]·we:¶
>
> •→ Achieved·an·almost·eleven-fold·increase·in·net·income·before·non-recurring§·XE· "non-recurring".§·items,·to·$10.9·million·from·$1·million·a·year·ago;¶
>
> •→ Completely·eliminated·our·long-term·debt§·XE·"debt"·§,·which·was·$10.2·million· last·fiscal·year;¶
>
> •→ Improved·our·stockholders'·equity§·XE·"equity"·§·to·$9·million·from·a·negative· net·worth·of·$24.3·million;¶

4. Insert and format the index.

a. In the **Navigation** pane, scroll down and navigate to the "Index" section.

b. Place the insertion point before the first paragraph mark below the title "Index."

c. On the **References** tab, in the **Index** group, click **Insert Index.**

d. In the **Index** dialog box, check **Right align page numbers.**

e. In the **Formats** drop-down list, verify that **From template** is selected. Click **Modify** to display the **Style** dialog box.

f. In the **Styles** list box, verify that **Index 1** is selected and click **Modify.**

g. In the **Modify Style** dialog box, in the **Formatting** section, from the Font drop-down list, select **Arial Narrow,** and click **OK.**

h. Click **OK** to close the **Style** dialog box.

i. Click **OK** to insert the index.

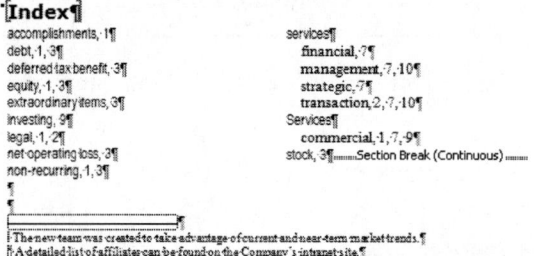

j. Save the file.

TOPIC C

Insert a Table of Figures

By adding an index, you made looking up content in a document easier. Similar functionality can be applied to the numerous figures in your document. In this topic, you will insert a table of figures.

Adding a table of figures to your long document is just another way to help readers find information quickly, especially if the document contains tables, figures, and illustrations. Instead of scrolling through the entire document, a table of figures provides a list of captions in the document and their corresponding page number. Word makes it easy to number and label figures and tables to create professional and easy-to-use documents.

The Table of Figures Dialog Box

The **Table of Figures** dialog box contains options to insert, format, and modify a table of figures.

Option	Enables You To
Print Preview	Preview the table of figures as it would appear in a printed Word document.
Web Preview	Preview the table of figures as it would appear on a web page.
Show page numbers	Display the page numbers in the table of figures.
Right align page numbers	Align the page numbers toward the right margin of the document.
Tab leader	Set tab leader formats for the page numbers.
Use hyperlinks instead of page numbers	Display the listed page references in the table of figures as hyperlinks so that the user can click a link to navigate to that particular page.
Formats	Format the table of figures.
Caption label	Insert a different caption label for the table of figures. You can choose whether to build a table of equations, a table of figures, or a table of tables. You can also choose (**none**) so that no label is included in the table.
Include label and number	Display the label and caption number in the table of figures.
Options	Display the **Table of Figures Options** dialog box. This dialog box consists of three options that enable you to specify the contents to be included as an entry in the table of figures. You can also specify a table identifier.
	• The **Style** drop-down list provides options that enable you to choose the type of style that is to be displayed in the table of figures.
	• The **Table entry fields** check box enables you to specify whether Word needs to use separate fields for identifying the different table of figures.
	• The **Table identifier** drop-down list enables you to set a table identifier code. The table identifier enables Word to identify the table of contents based on hierarchy.

Option	Enables You To
Modify	Display the **Style** dialog box that enables you to modify the style of the table of figures.

Other Types of Reference Tables

The **Caption label** drop-down list in the **Table of Figures** dialog box enables you to create other types of reference tables. Choosing the **Table** option from the **Caption label** drop-down list enables you to create a table of tables. Likewise, to create a table of equations, you can choose the **Equation** option from the **Caption label** drop-down list.

 While adding a caption to an object, you have the option to select the caption label as figures, tables, or equations. When you want to build a table of figures, table of tables, or table of equations, Word populates this information based on the label selected for the caption.

How to Insert a Table of Figures

Procedure Reference: Insert a Table of Figures

To insert a table of figures:

1. Place the insertion point where you want the table of figures to be located.
2. On the **References** tab, in the **Captions** group, click **Insert Table of Figures.**
3. In the **Table of Figures** dialog box, specify the desired options.
4. If necessary, click **Options** and specify the desired settings in the **Table of Figures Options** dialog box.
5. If necessary, click **Modify** and specify the desired settings.
    a. In the **Style** dialog box, select the table of figure style you want to change and click **Modify.**
    b. In the **Modify Style** dialog box, modify the style as desired and click **OK.**
    c. If necessary, modify other table of figures styles.
    d. Click **OK** to close the **Modify** dialog box.
6. Click **OK** to insert the table of figures.
7. If necessary, in the **Microsoft Word** message box, click **OK** to update an existing table of figures.

Procedure Reference: Update a Table of Figures

To update a table of figures:

1. In the document window, display the table of figures you want to update.
2. Display the **Update Table of Figures** dialog box.
    - On the **References** tab, in the **Captions** group, click **Update Table.**
    - Or, right-click the table of figures and choose **Update Field.**
    - Or, place the insertion point in the table and press **F9.**

3.   Select the desired update option.

- Select the **Update page numbers only** option to update only the page numbers in the table of figures.
- Select the **Update entire table** option to update the entire table along with page numbers.

4.   Click **OK** to update the table of figures.

ACTIVITY 5-3
Inserting a Table of Figures

Before You Begin:

My Annual Report With Tables.docx is open.

Scenario:

Scanning through a report, you feel that locating information in it would be a lot easier if you added a reference table for figures and tables.

---

1. Insert a table of figures below the "Figures" heading.

    a. Display the **Bookmark** dialog box.

    b. In the **Bookmark** dialog box, select the **Figures** bookmark name and click **Go To**.

    c. Click **Close** to close the **Bookmark** dialog box.

    d. Place the insertion point in the blank line below the heading "Figures."

    e. On the **References** tab, in the **Captions** group, click **Insert Table of Figures**.

    f. In the **Table of Figures** dialog box, in the **General** section, in the **Formats** drop-down list, verify that **From template** is selected and, in the **Caption label** drop-down list, select **Figure**.

    g. Click **Options** to display the **Table of Figures Options** dialog box.

    h. From the **Table identifier** drop-down list, select **A** and click **OK**.

    i. Click **OK** to insert the table of figures.

    > **⌊Figures¶**
    > Figure·A:·Teamwork·is·critical·to·our·success.................→........................2¶
    > Figure·B:·Southern·home·sales·remain·strong.................→........................4¶
    > Figure·C:·The·Relocation·management·team....................→........................6¶

---

2. Modify the table of figures.

    a. Display the **Table of Figures** dialog box.

    b. In the **Table of Figures** dialog box, in the **Caption label** drop-down list, select **Figure**.

    c. Click **Modify** to display the **Style** dialog box.

    d. In the **Style** dialog box, in the **Preview** section, click **Modify.**

    e. In the **Modify Style** dialog box, from the Font drop-down list, select **Arial Narrow**.

    f. Click **OK** three times to close all open dialog boxes.

    g. In the **Microsoft Word** message box, click **Yes** to update the existing table of figures.

h. Observe that the font of the text in the table of figures is changed to Arial Narrow.

3. Insert references for all tables.

    a. Place the insertion point in the blank line below the heading "Tables."

    b. Display the **Table of Figures** dialog box.

    c. In the **Caption label** drop-down list, verify that **Table** is selected.

    d. Click **OK** to insert the table of tables.

Tables¶

Table·1:·The·North·regularly·lags·behind..............................→............................4¶

    e. Save the document.

ACTIVITY 5-4

Updating a Table of Figures

Before You Begin:

My Annual Report With Tables.docx is open.

Scenario:

Your manager approves the annual report you created. However, she has asked you to change the caption for Figure C and update the table of figures accordingly.

---

1. Update the figure caption.

   a. In the table of figures, Ctrl-click the text **"Figure C: The Relocation management team."**

   b. In the Figure C caption, place the insertion point after the text "Relocation," press the **Spacebar** and type *Services*

---

2. Update the table of figures.

   a. Display the **Bookmark** dialog box.

   b. In the **Bookmark name** list box, select **Figures,** click **Go To** and close the **Bookmark** dialog box.

   c. Right-click the table of figures and choose **Update Field.**

   d. In the **Update Table of Figures** dialog box, select the **Update entire table** option and click **OK** to update the table of figures with the text inserted in the caption.

   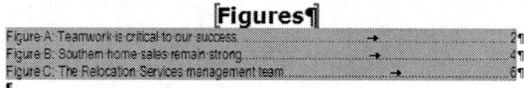

   e. Save the document.

TOPIC D

Insert a Table of Authorities

So far, you inserted a table of figures to help readers locate illustrations and other special contents in your document. Locating legal citations in a long document is as challenging as locating specific figures. Consequently, it is in your readers' best interests for you to identify each citation and list them in a table. In this topic, you will insert a table of authorities.

Assume that you are in a courtroom and want to refer to a legal precedent in a document. Locating a specific legal citation in a long document can be a very tedious and time consuming task. A table of authorities provides a way to locate legal citations quickly. By using Word to insert a table of authorities, you are ensuring that the table of authorities will be up-to-date whenever a document's text or pagination changes.

The Mark Citation Dialog Box

The **Mark Citation** dialog box contains options to mark the required citations before inserting a table of authorities.

Option	Description
Selected text	Displays the citation text as a selection.
Category	Displays a list of categories that applies to the citation.
Short citation	Enables you to insert a citation in the document and also help Word use this citation as a way to locate and mark other related citations.
Long citation	Displays the details of the source for the selected citation.
Next Citation	Enables you to navigate to the next citation in the document.
Mark	Enables you to mark the selected citation as an entry for the table of authorities.
Mark All	Enables you to mark all citations similar to the one entered as a main entry.
Category	Displays the **Edit Category** dialog box. This dialog box provides options that help replace a selected category of authority with another.

The Table of Authorities Dialog Box

The **Table of Authorities** dialog box contains options to insert, format, and modify a table of authorities.

Option	Description
Print Preview	Displays a preview to show how the table of authorities appears in a printed document.
Category	Displays a list of categories that you want to include in your table of authorities.
Use passim	Displays the word **passim** next to the citation entry if the same citation has been inserted more than five times.

Option	Description
Keep original formatting	Replicates the format of the marked citations in the table of authorities, thus preventing formatting discrepancies from being created.
Tab leader	Enables you to set tab leader formats for the page numbers in the table of authorities.
Formats	Enables you to format the table of authorities.
Mark Citation	Displays the **Mark Citation** dialog box that can be used to mark additional citations to be inserted in the table of authorities.
Modify	Displays the **Style** dialog box that enables you to modify the style of the table of authorities.

The Use Passim Option

In the **Table of Authorities** dialog box, the **Use passim** check box is checked by default. Passim means "occurs frequently." If there are five or more page references to the same marked legal citation, Word will insert the word "passim" in the table rather than the page numbers when the table of authorities is inserted.

How to Insert a Table of Authorities

Procedure Reference: Mark Text for a Table of Authorities

To mark text for a table of authorities:

1. Navigate to and select the desired citation.
2. Display the **Mark Citation** dialog box.
    *   On the **References** tab, in the **Table Of Authorities** group, click **Mark Citation.**
    *   In the **Table of Authorities** dialog box, click **Mark Citation.**
    *   Or, press **Alt+Shift+I.**
3. If necessary, in the **Selected text** text box, modify the citation.
4. If necessary, from the **Category** drop-down list, select the category that applies to the selected caption.
5. In the **Short citation** text box, edit the citation so that it matches how you use the citation elsewhere in the document. Entering a citation in the **Short citation** text box helps Word use this citation to locate and mark other related citations.
6. Mark the citation.
    *   Click **Mark** to mark the selected citation.
    *   Or, click **Mark All** to mark all instances of that citation in the document.

 Word doesn't mark multiple criteria in the same paragraph.

7. Click **Close.**

8. If necessary, modify the marked citation.

    a. If necessary, display the formatting marks in the document.

    b. Navigate to the citation you want to modify.

    c. In the citation's **TA** field code, edit the long citation text within the quotation marks.

9. If necessary, delete the marked citation.

    a. If necessary, display the formatting marks.

    b. Select the field codes for the desired marked citation.

    c. Press **Delete.**

Field Codes for a Marked Citation

When you mark a citation as a table of authorities entry, Word inserts a field code that resembles { TA \l "Connor v. OGC, 314 US 252 (2008)" \s "Connor v. OGC" \c 1}. The "\l" indicates the **Long citation,** the "\s" indicates the **Short citation,** and "\c" indicates the **Cases** category.

Procedure Reference: Insert a Table of Authorities

To insert a table of authorities:

1. Place the insertion point where you want to insert the table.

2. On the **References** tab, in the **Table of Authorities** group, click the **Insert Table of Authorities** button.

3. In the **Table of Authorities** dialog box, on the **Table of Authorities** tab, set the desired settings.

    ● From the **Formats** drop-down list, select an available default format to apply to the table of authorities.

    ● From the **Tab leader** drop-down list, select the desired style for tab leaders.

    ● Click **Modify** to display the **Style** dialog box and specify the style for the table entries.

        ■ From the **Styles** list box, select a style for the table entries.

        ■ Click **Modify,** and in the **Modify Style** dialog box, specify the settings to modify a style and set the alignment options for the style applied to the table entries

4. If necessary, click **Mark Citations** and mark more citations.

5. If necessary, modify the appearance of the table.

6. Click **OK** to insert the table of authorities.

7. If necessary, in the **Microsoft Word** message box, click **OK** to update the existing table.

 A table of authorities does not provide a hyperlink option. Therefore, the user cannot use Ctrl-click to navigate to the citation.

Procedure Reference: Update a Table of Authorities

To update a table of authorities:

1. Navigate to the table of authorities.

2. Update the table of authorities.
   - Right-click the table and choose **Update Field.**
   - Place the insertion point in the table of authorities and press **F9.**
   - Or, on the **References** tab, in the **Table of Authorities** group, click the **Update Table of Authorities** button.

ACTIVITY 5-5
Inserting a Table of Authorities

Before You Begin:
My Annual Report With Tables.docx is open.

Scenario:
You are sending a report to the legal team in your firm. The report contains a couple of citations to legal cases involving the company. You need to provide an easy way to refer to those citations.

---

1. Mark all instances of the Connor v. OGC case.

    a. Using the **Navigation** pane, navigate to the heading "Legal Issues."

    b. Select the text "Connor v. OGC, 314 US 252 (2008)."

    c. On the **References** tab, in the **Table of Authorities** group, click **Mark Citation.**

    d. In the **Mark Citation** dialog box, in the **Category** drop-down list, verify that **Cases** is selected.

    e. In the **Short citation** text box, type *Connor v. OGC*

    f. Click **Mark All.**

    g. Close the **Mark Citation** dialog box and scroll up to view the complete citation.

    h. Notice that the citation is followed by the field code: { TA \1 "Connor v. OGC, 314 US 252 (2008)" \s "Connor v. OGC" \c 1 }.

    > ·**Legal**{·XE·"legal"·}·**Issues**¶
    > On·the·legal{·XE·"legal"·}·front,·*Connor·v.·OGC*,·314·US·252·(2008){·TA·\l·"*Connor·v.·OGC*,·314·US·252·(2008)"·\s·"Connor·v.·OGC"·\c·1·}·and·*Smith·v.·OGC*,·F2d·201·(2009)·have·been·dismissed.·The·primary·reason·for·dismissal·in·both·decisions·was·the·lack·of·evidence·on·the·part·of·the·prosecution.·However,·this·does·raise·an·interesting·question.·

---

2. Mark all instances of the Smith v. OGC case.

    a. In the "Legal Issues" paragraph, select the text "Smith v. OGC, F2d 201 (2009)."

    b. Display the **Mark Citation** dialog box.

    c. In the **Short citation** text box, type *Smith v. OGC* and click **Mark All.**

    d. Close the **Mark Citation** dialog box and scroll up to view the complete citation.

    > ·**Legal**{·XE·"legal"·}·**Issues**¶
    > On·the·legal{·XE·"legal"·}·front,·*Connor·v.·OGC*,·314·US·252·(2008){·TA·\l·"*Connor·v.·OGC*,·314·US·252·(2008)"·\s·"Connor·v.·OGC"·\c·1·}·and·*Smith·v.·OGC*,·F2d·201·(2009){·TA·\l·"*Smith·v.·OGC*,·F2d·201·(2009)"·\s·"Smith·v.·OGC"·\c·1·}·have·been·dismissed.·The·primary·reason·for·dismissal·in·both·decisions·was·the·lack·of·evidence·

---

3. Insert a table of authorities below the "Authorities" heading.

   a. Display the **Bookmark** dialog box.

   b. In the **Bookmark name** list box, select **Authorities** and click **Go To.**

   c. Click **Close** to close the **Bookmark** dialog box.

   d. Place the insertion point in the blank line below the heading "Authorities."

   e. On the **References** tab, in the **Table of Authorities** group, click the **Insert Table of Authorities** button.

   f. In the **Table of Authorities** dialog box, in the **Category** list box, select **Cases.**

   g. In the **Formats** drop-down list, verify that **From template** is selected and click **OK** to insert the table of authorities.

Authorities¶

Cases¶
Cornor·v.·OGC,·314·US·252·(2008).................................→.................................1,·2¶
Smith·v.·OGC,·F2d·201·(2009).................................→.................................1,·2,·4¶

   h. Save the document.

ACTIVITY 5-6
Modifying a Table of Authorities

Before You Begin:
My Annual Report With Tables.docx is open.

Scenario:
The reviewer has sent you the annual report, pointing out that the Connor vs. OGC case took place in 2009 not 2008. Also, the formatting is inconsistent in the table. He suggests that the table's text be formatted similar to the one in other reference tables of the document.

---

1. Edit the information for the Connor vs. OGC case.

   a. Using the **Navigation** pane, navigate to the heading "Legal Issues."

   b. In the first paragraph below the "Legal Issues" heading, in the third line, change both occurrences of the text (2008) to *(2009)*

---

2. Update the table of authorities to reflect the change in year.

   a. Display the **Bookmark** dialog box, navigate to the **Authorities** bookmark.

   b. Right-click the table of authorities and choose **Update Field.**

   c. Observe that the content has been updated.

---

3. Format the table of authorities.

   a. Display the **Table of Authorities** dialog box.

   b. Click **Modify** to display the **Style** dialog box.

   c. In the **Styles** list box, select **Table of Authorities** and then click **Modify.**

   d. In the **Modify Style** dialog box, in the **Formatting** section, from the Font drop-down list, select **Arial Narrow.**

   e. Click **OK** three times to close all the open dialog boxes.

   f. In the **Microsoft Word** message box, click **OK** to update the existing table of authorities.

   g. Save the document.

TOPIC E
Insert a Table of Contents

In the previous topic, you inserted a table of authorities to help readers locate legal information in a document. The last major type of reference table you are likely to include in your document is a table of contents, which will serve as a comprehensive list for the entire document. In this topic, you will insert a table of contents into a document.

Most people don't read reference books cover to cover, so you know the importance of including a table of contents. A table of contents helps your readers to quickly find the topics they want. And, like other reference tables in Word, a table of contents remains up-to-date whenever the document's text or pagination changes.

Table of Contents

A table of contents (TOC) is a list of headings with corresponding page numbers. You can format the text in a document by using heading styles such as Heading 1, Heading 2, and Heading 3. Applying predefined heading styles to different pieces of text in a document enables Word to identify and list the headings at different levels when creating a table of contents.

The Table of Contents Dialog Box

The **Table of Contents** dialog box contains options to insert, format, and modify a table of contents.

Option	Enables You To
Print Preview	Preview how the table of contents appears in a printed Word document.
Web Preview	Preview how the table of contents appears in a web page.
Show page numbers	Display the page numbers in the table of contents.
Right align page numbers	Align the page numbers toward the right margin of a document.
Tab leader	Set tab leader formats for the page numbers.
Use hyperlinks instead of page numbers	Preview the listed page references in the table of contents as hyperlinks so that users can click a desired link to navigate to a particular page.
Formats	Format the table of contents.
Show levels	Determine the level of listing in the table of contents.

Option	Enables You To
Options	Display the **Table of Contents Options** dialog box. This dialog box contains three options that enable users to modify the style and listing of the table of contents.
	• The **Available styles** section displays a list of options from which users can choose to include styles beside the standard heading styles and also determine the level of listing.
	• The **Outline levels** option enables users to modify the selected style's outline level in the **Paragraph** dialog box.
	• The **Table entry fields** option updates the field codes automatically to mark hierarchy.
Modify	Display the **Style** dialog box that enables users to modify the style of the table of contents.

The Add Text Option

After selecting the text you want to add to the table of contents, you can choose its level of hierarchy using the options in the **Add Text** drop-down list.

Option	Description
Do Not Show in Table of Contents	Does not display the text among the headings in the table of contents.
Level 1	Displays the selected text at the first level of the hierarchy.
Level 2	Displays the selected text at the second level of the hierarchy.
Level 3	Displays the selected text at the third level of the hierarchy.

The Mark Table of Contents Entry Dialog Box

The **Mark Table of Contents Entry** dialog box contains options to manually mark text as an entry for the table of contents.

Option	Description
Entry	Displays the text that is to be marked as an entry for the table of contents.
Table identifier	Enables Word to identify the table of contents based on hierarchy.
Level	Enables the user to select a level for the table of contents entry.
Mark	Marks the text with the specified settings as an entry for the table of contents.

How to Insert a Table of Contents

Procedure Reference: Insert a Table of Contents

To insert a table of contents using the **Table of Contents** dialog box:

1. Insert the headings in your document's outline that you want to automatically include in the table of contents.

2. Format the headings with the appropriate styles so that the table of contents can be generated.

3. Mark other entries for the table of contents manually.

   a. Select the desired content.

   b. Press **Alt+Shift+O** to display the **Mark Table of Contents Entry** dialog box.

   c. If necessary, in the **Entry** text box, edit the entry text.

   d. If necessary, from the **Table identifier** drop-down list, select the table identifier.

   e. If necessary, in the **Level** spin box, mark a level of listing for the selected text.

   f. Click **Mark.**

4. Place the insertion point where you want the table of contents to be located.

5. On the **References** tab, in the **Table of Contents** group, from the **Table of Contents** drop-down list, select **Insert Table of Contents.**

6. In the **Table of Contents** dialog box, specify the desired settings.

   - Check **Show page numbers** to display the page numbers in the table of contents entries.

   - Align the page numbers.

     - Check **Right-align page numbers** to align the page numbers to the right.

     - From the **Tab leader** drop-down list, select the desired tab leader.

   - Check **Use hyperlinks instead of page numbers** to insert the reference as a hyperlink.

   - If necessary, from the **Formats** drop-down list, select a default format for the table of contents design.

   - If necessary, in the **Show level** spin box, specify the level settings.

7. If necessary, change the style settings for the table.

8. If necessary, modify the appearance of the table.

9. Click **OK** to insert the table of contents.

Procedure Reference: Update a Table of Contents

To update a table of contents:

1. Navigate to the desired table of contents.

2. Display the **Update Table of Contents** dialog box.

   - Right-click the table and choose **Update Field.**

   - Place the insertion point in the table of contents and press **F9.**

   - On the **References** tab, in the **Table of Contents** group, click **Update Table.**

   - Or, press **Alt+S+U.**

3. Specify the desired update option.

- Select **Update page numbers only** to update the page numbers in the table.
- Select **Update entire table** to update the content and page numbers in the table.

4. Click **OK** to update the table.

 If you change the formatting or text entries in a table of contents directly and then update the table using the **Update Table of Contents** dialog box, the changes made will be lost. However, if you first make changes to the contents in the document and then update the table, the table of contents would be updated.

Procedure Reference: Add Entries to the Table of Contents

To add entries manually to the table of contents:

1. In the document, select the text you wish to add to the table.
2. On the **References** tab, in the **Table of Contents** group, from the **Add Text** drop-down list, select the desired level of listing.
3. Update the table of contents.

ACTIVITY 5-7
Inserting a Table of Contents

Before You Begin:

My Annual Report With Tables.docx is open.

Scenario:

You have written a comprehensive company guide that will be distributed to all of your company's current employees. You want to provide an accurate table of contents to make it easier for the employees to quickly access the information they need. And because the document contains text formatted with the Heading 1, Heading 2, and Heading 3 styles already, it shouldn't be difficult. Also, in the table of contents, text should be formatted in a way that's similar to text in the other reference tables.

---

1. Set options for a two-level table of contents.

   a. Using the **Bookmark** dialog box, navigate to the **Contents** bookmark and then close the dialog box.

   b. Place the insertion point in the blank line after the heading "Contents."

   c. On the **References** tab, in the **Table of Contents** group, click the **Table of Contents** drop-down and select **Insert Table of Contents.**

   d. In the **Table of Contents** dialog box, in the **General** section, in the **Formats** drop-down list, verify that **From template** is selected.

   e. In the **Show levels** spin box, set the level listing to 2.

---

2. Format the table of contents.

   a. In the **Table of Contents** dialog box, click **Modify.**

   b. In the **Style** dialog box, in the **Styles** list box, verify that **TOC 1** is selected and click **Modify.**

   c. In the **Modify Style** dialog box, in the **Formatting** section, from the Font drop-down list, select **Arial Narrow** and click **OK** to close the **Modify Style** dialog box.

   d. Click **OK** two times to close the open dialog boxes and to insert the table of contents.

e. Observe that the table of contents is inserted based on the Heading 1 text style and formatted with the Arial Narrow font face.

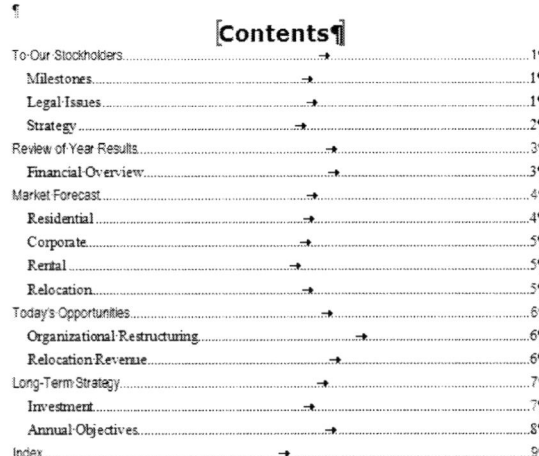

f. Save the document and close it.

TOPIC F

Create a Master Document

Throughout this lesson, you have inserted various reference tables in your long documents to access information more easily. An alternative would be to work with shorter documents and combine them later. In this topic, you will create a master document that consists of several subdocuments.

The longer a document gets, the more complicated it can be to work with, especially when several people are collaborating on it. Rather than trying to wrestle with a huge document, creating a master document is a more manageable solution because it will act as a container for several smaller documents.

Master Documents

Definition:

A *master document* is a document that contains links to other related documents called subdocuments. You can use a master document to organize and maintain a long document by dividing it into smaller, more manageable subdocuments. The master document can contain links to any number of subdocuments. The contents can be modified either in the individual subdocuments or in the master document with those changes being reflected dynamically in the other location.

Example:

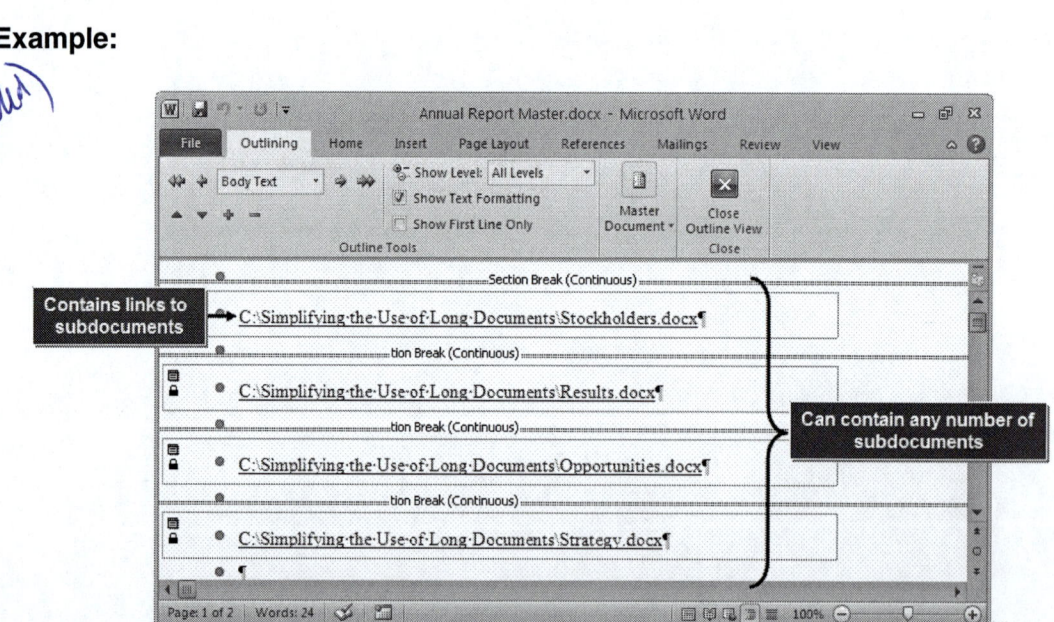

Figure 5-2: The contents of linked subdocuments are displayed in the master document.

Benefits of Master Documents

Using a master document, you can separate a long document into shorter, more manageable pieces of subdocuments. Subdocuments may be easier for you to rearrange within the master document rather than cutting and pasting or dragging sections around in **Outline** view. Master documents have additional benefits, such as:

● Allowing for quicker compilation of documents in a central location for easier access.

- Providing a convenient means to mark entries and insert referential tables for several documents.

- Reducing the file size because the master document doesn't actually contain the subdocument content; rather, it contains the link to the subdocuments.

- Allowing for printing of multiple documents without opening them individually.

Deleting Subdocument Links from the Main Document

Deleting the link to the subdocument from the master document will remove the link to the subdocument from the master document, but not the content in the subdocument. To delete the link to the subdocument, display the master document in **Outline** view, click the subdocument icon to select it and then press **Delete** to delete the subdocument.

Master Document Group

The **Master Document** group contains options that help you to work with master documents. Options in this group are visible only on clicking the **Show Document** button.

Option	Description
Show Document	Displays the other options in the **Master Document** group.
Collapse Subdocuments/ Expand Subdocuments	Acts as a toggle to choose between showing the full path to the subdocument file or the actual subdocument content.
Create	Creates a new subdocument.
Insert	Inserts an existing file as a subdocument.
Unlink	Deletes the link to the subdocument and copies the subdocument content into the master document.
Merge	Combines the content of two or more subdocuments in the master document into one subdocument.
Split	Splits the content of the subdocument in the master document into two or more subdocuments.
Lock Document	Locks or unlocks a subdocument so that modification to the content in the master document is not propagated to the subdocuments.

 You can also lock the subdocuments to prevent other users from modifying the content.

How to Create a Master Document

Procedure Reference: Create a Master Document

To create a master document:

1. Open a new document and save it in the .docx format.

2. Display the document in **Outline** view.

    ●   On the **View** tab, in the **Document Views** group, click **Outline.**

    ●   Or, on the Microsoft Office Status Bar, click the **Outline** button.

3. In the **Master Document** group, click **Show Document.**

4. Place the insertion point where you want to insert the subdocument.

5. Click **Insert** and navigate to and open the desired document to add it into the master document as a subdocument. Word creates section breaks before and after the content of the subdocument(s) in the master document.

6. Add other subdocuments as per your requirements.

7. If necessary, use the options in the **Outline Tools** group to format the content of the subdocument(s) in the master document.

 Any modification made to the content of the subdocument in the master document is reflected in the respective subdocument itself.

8. If necessary, use the options in the **Master Document** group to work with the master document.

9. In the **Close** group, click **Close Outline View** to close the outline view and return to editing the document.

10. Save the master document.

Procedure Reference: Modify the Master Document

To modify the master document:

1. On the **Outlining** tab, in the **Master Document** group, click **Show Document.**

2. Use the options in the **Outline Tools** group to format the content of the subdocument(s) in the master document.

3. Use the options in the **Master Document** group to work with the master document.

4. If necessary, click the subdocument icon to the left of the subdocument to select it and then press **Delete** to delete it from the master document.

 Deleting a subdocument from the master document only removes the link to the subdocument and not the subdocument itself.

Delinking Subdocuments

Once a subdocument has been inserted into the master, it becomes linked to the master and its contents can be edited directly in the master. All changes made to the subdocument in the master document are saved to the subdocument. To remove the connection between the subdocument and its content in the master document, click the corresponding subdocument's icon and then click the **Remove Subdocument** button.

ACTIVITY 5-8
Creating a Master Document

Data Files:

C:\084584Data\Simplifying the Use of Long Documents\Annual Report Master.docx,
C:\084584Data\Simplifying the Use of Long Documents\Stockholders.docx, C:\084584Data\
Simplifying the Use of Long Documents\Results.docx, C:\084584Data\Simplifying the Use of
Long Documents\Forecast.docx, C:\084584Data\Simplifying the Use of Long Documents\
Opportunities.docx, C:\084584Data\Simplifying the Use of Long Documents\Strategy.docx

Before You Begin:

To retain a copy of the original Stockholders document, make a copy of the document and
suffix it with your student ID.

Scenario:

You are constantly updating the annual report and its supporting documents. Rather than making changes in two places, you want to combine the supporting documents into a single
document container so that whenever you make any changes in one place, they are reflected in
the other. This will also make it easier to update any existing reference tables and indices, as
needed.

---

1. Insert the Stockholders document as a subdocument in the Annual Report Master docu-
    ment.

    a. From the C:\084584Data\Simplifying the Use of Long Documents folder, open the
        Annual Report Master.docx file.

    b. Scroll down to page 2 and place the insertion point at the beginning of the page.

    c. On the status bar, click the **Outline** button.

    d. On the **Outlining** tab, in the **Master Document** group, click **Show Document** to dis-
        play the additional options in the group.

    e. In the **Master Document** group, click **Insert.**

    f. In the **Insert Subdocument** dialog box, select the Stockholders document and click
        Open.

    g. Observe that the content of the Stockholders document is added.

---

2. Insert the other supporting documents as subdocuments below the Stockholders subdocu-
    ment.

    a. Verify that the insertion point is at the end of the Stockholders document content.

    b. On the **Outlining** tab, in the **Master Document** group, click **Insert.**

    c. Open the Results document.

> d. Similarly add the Forecast, Opportunities, and Strategy documents as subdocuments.
>
> e. Save the master document as ***My Annual Report Master***

3. Verify that all subdocuments have been inserted.

> a. On the **Outlining** tab, in the **Master Document** group, click **Collapse Subdocuments.**
>
> b. Observe that the path and file names for the subdocuments are indicated as links.

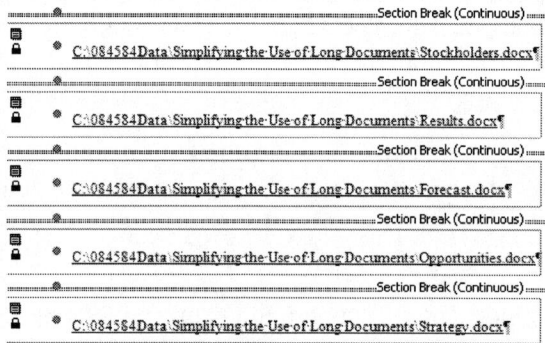

4. Test the master document.

> a. Ctrl-click the first link to open the Stockholders subdocument.
>
> b. Close the Stockholders document.

ACTIVITY 5-9
Modifying the Master Document

Before You Begin:

My Annual Report Master.docx is open.

Scenario:

You sent the master document for review to your manager. She sent the document back to you asking you to change the Strategy heading in the Strategy subdocument to Policy. She also requested you to delete the Forecast document.

---

1. Modify the heading "Strategy."

   a. On the **Outlining** tab, in the **Master Document** group, click **Expand Subdocuments.**

   b. On the status bar, click the **Print Layout** button.

   c. Using the **Navigation** pane, navigate to the heading "Strategy."

   d. Select the word "Strategy" in the heading and type **Policy**

---

2. Verify that the change is reflected in the Stockholders document.

   a. Display the **Open** dialog box.

   b. From the C:\084584Data\Simplifying the Use of Long Documents folder, open the Stockholders document.

   c. Using the **Navigation** pane, navigate to the "Policy" heading. Observe that the heading has been changed from "Strategy" to "Policy." Close the Stockholders document.

---

3. In the master document, delete the Forecast subdocument.

   a. Using the **Navigation** pane, navigate to the heading "Market Forecast."

   b. On the status bar, click the **Outline** button.

   c. To the left of the "Market Forecast" heading, click the subdocument icon ⊕ to select the subdocument.

   d. Press **Delete** to delete the subdocument.

   e. On the **Outlining** tab, in the **Master Document** group, click **Collapse Subdocuments.**

   f. In the **Microsoft Word** message box, click **OK** to save the document.

g. Observe that the link to the Forecast subdocument is removed from the master document.

```
.......................................................Section Break (Continuous) .........
  ⊕ C:\084584Data\Simplifying-the-Use-of-Long-Documents\Stockholders.docx¶
.......................................................Section Break (Continuous) .........
  ⊕ C:\084584Data\Simplifying-the-Use-of-Long-Documents\Results.docx¶
.......................................................Section Break (Continuous) .........
  ⊕ C:\084584Data\Simplifying-the-Use-of-Long-Documents\Opportunities.docx¶
.......................................................Section Break (Continuous) .........
  ⊕ C:\084584Data\Simplifying-the-Use-of-Long-Documents\Strategy.docx¶
  ⊕ ¶
```

h. On the **Outlining** tab, in the **Close** group, click **Close Outline View** to close the outline view.

i. Close the **Navigation** pane.

j. Save and close the document.

Lesson 5 Follow-up

In this lesson, you used the various features of Word to help simplify the use of long documents. You marked text as an index entry; added tables of figures, authorities, and contents; and, created a master document.

1. **What types of long documents do you create at work?**

2. **Which of the techniques discussed in this lesson would add value to your printed documents and make them reader-friendly?**

6 | Securing a Document

Lesson Time: 1 hour(s)

Lesson Objectives:

In this lesson, you will secure a document.

You will:

- Hide text.
- Remove personal information from a document.
- Set formatting and editing restrictions for a document.
- Add a digital signature to a document.
- Use a password to open a document.
- Restrict document access.

Introduction

Now that your document is complete with a table of contents and other table references, you may want to distribute it. But, before that, you may need to prevent unauthorized access or changes to the contents in the document. In this lesson, you will secure a document.

When working on restricted content, such as a report on legal cases involving your company, you need to ensure that no one but authorized people have access to it. The security features in Word enable you to protect a document and its contents.

TOPIC A

Hide Text

You have added table references in your document to help other readers. However, a document may have information that should not be made public or seen by others. In this topic, you will hide text.

In today's business environment, preventing proprietary or personal data from becoming public is very important. One of the best ways to keep information private is by hiding it. Word allows you to hide text in your document, and the text will not appear unless you opt to display it.

How to Hide Text

Procedure Reference: Hide Text in a Document

To hide text in a document:

1. If necessary, show the nonprinting characters.

   - On the **Home** tab, in the **Paragraph** group, click the **Show/Hide** button.
   - Or, show the nonprinting characters using the **Word Options** dialog box.

      a. Display the **Word Options** dialog box.

      b. In the left pane, select the **Display** category.

      c. In the **Always show these formatting marks on the screen** section, check **Show all formatting marks**, and click **OK.**

2. Select the text to be hidden.

3. On the **Home** tab, in the **Font** group, click the **Dialog Box Launcher** button to display the **Font** dialog box.

4. In the **Effects** section, check **Hidden** and click **OK.**

5. On the **Home** tab, click the **Show/Hide** button to hide the selected text. When formatting marks are hidden, the selected text is automatically hidden.

6. If necessary, print the hidden text.

   a. Display the **Display** category in the **Word Options** dialog box.

   b. In the **Printing options** section, check **Print hidden text,** and click **OK.**

   c. Select the **File** tab and choose **Print.**

   d. In the **Print** section, specify the desired options, and click **Print.**

ACTIVITY 6-1
Hiding Text in a Document

Data Files:

C:\084584Data\Securing a Document\Stockholder Insert.docx

Scenario:

The company's marketing manager wants to create a document from the annual report's "To Our Stockholders" section. He wants the document to be precise and display only the necessary information, hiding the company's legal issues from potential clients.

---

1. Hide the "To Our Stockholders" heading.

    a. From the C:\084584Data\Securing a Document folder, open the Stockholder Insert.docx file.

    b. Select the "To Our Stockholders" heading.

    · To·Our·Stockholders¶

    · *Milestones*¶

    c. On the **Home** tab, in the **Font** group, click the **Font** dialog box launcher to display the **Font** dialog box.

    d. In the **Font** dialog box, on the **Font** tab, in the **Effects** section, check **Hidden** and click **OK.**

    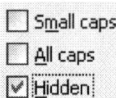

    e. Observe that the text is underlined indicating that its property has been changed to **Hidden.**

---

2. Hide the paragraphs below the "Milestones" heading.

    a. Under the "Milestones" heading, select the paragraph that begins with "This fiscal year..."

    b. Display the **Font** dialog box.

    c. Check **Hidden** and click **OK.**

    d. Scroll down, and below the bulleted list, select the paragraph that begins with "To put the year..."

    e. Display the **Font** dialog box.

f. Check **Hidden** and click **OK.**

3. Hide the "Legal Issues" section.

a. Select the "Legal Issues" heading and the two paragraphs below it.

b. Display the **Font** dialog box.

c. Check **Hidden** and click **OK.**

d. On the **Home** tab, in the **Paragraph** group, click the **Show/Hide** button.

e. Notice that all the underlined text is now hidden.

f. Save the document as *My Stockholder Insert* and close it.

TOPIC B

Remove Personal Information from a Document

You now are able to hide information in a document. However, hiding content may not prevent others from viewing it. In this topic, you will remove personal information from a document altogether.

Sometimes, you may get calls or mails raising queries about a document that you created years ago. You may wonder why people keep calling you. It's because you originally created the document and your name is still there in the Author field of the document's properties. If you save documents without your personal information, you can avoid these calls.

The Document Inspector Dialog Box

The **Document Inspector** dialog box provides you with various options to identify specific content in a document.

Option	*Description*
Comments, Revisions, Versions, and Annotations	Inspects the document for comments, versions, revision marks, and ink annotations.
Document Properties and Personal Information	Inspects for hidden metadata and personal information saved in a document.
Custom XML Data	Inspects for custom XML data stored with a document.
Headers, Footers, and Watermarks	Inspects the document for information on the header, footer, and watermark.
Invisible Content	Inspects the document for objects that have been formatted as invisible.
Hidden Text	Inspects the document for text that has been formatted as hidden.

How to Remove Personal Information from a Document

Procedure Reference: Delete Custom Properties

To delete custom properties:

1. Display the document Properties dialog box.

2. Select the **Custom** tab.

3. In the **Properties** list box, select the custom property you want to remove, click **Delete,** and click **OK** to close the dialog box.

Procedure Reference: Remove Personal Information Using the Document Inspector

To remove personal information using the **Document Inspector:**

1. If necessary, open the document from which you want to remove the personal information.

2. On the **File** tab, in the **Prepare for Sharing** section, choose **Check for Issues→Inspect Document.**

3. In the **Document Inspector** dialog box, check **Document Properties and Personal Information** and click **Inspect.**

4. Review the results of the inspection.

5. If necessary, next to the inspection results, click **Remove All** to remove the document properties and personal information from the document.

6. Click **Close.**

ACTIVITY 6-2
Removing Personal Information from a Document

Data Files:

C:\084584Data\Securing a Document\Annual Report.docx

Scenario:

You are ready to send the annual report for printing. However, before you email the document to the printers, you need to ensure that it is devoid of personal information.

---

1. Remove the custom value specified for the Editor property.

   a. From the C:\084584Data\Securing a Document folder, open the Annual Report.docx file.

   b. Display the Backstage view.

   c. Display the **Annual Report.docx Properties** dialog box.

   d. In the **Annual Report.docx Properties** dialog box, select the **Custom** tab.

   e. On the **Custom** tab, in the **Properties** list box, select **Editor**, which shows Mary Coleman as the value.

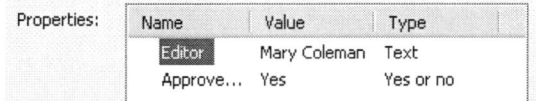

   f. Click **Delete** and then click **OK.**

   g. Save the document as *My Annual Report*

---

2. Remove all personal information using the **Document Inspector.**

   a. Select the **File** tab, and in the Backstage view, in the **Prepare for Sharing** section, choose **Check for Issues→Inspect Document.**

   b. In the **Document Inspector** dialog box, uncheck all check boxes other than **Document Properties and Personal Information.**

   c. Click **Inspect.**

   d. Notice the results of the inspection and click **Remove All** to remove all personal information from your document.

   e. Observe that the **Document Inspector** dialog box indicates that the document properties and personal information were successfully removed. Click **Close.**

   f. Save and close the document.

TOPIC C
Set Formatting and Editing Restrictions

You know how to remove personal information from a document. But, sometimes that measure alone is not enough to protect your documents. To preserve the authenticity of your document, you will need to prevent others from changing and formatting its contents. In this topic, you will specify formatting and editing restrictions for a given document.

When you share a document with others, you may want them to focus on the contents of the document and not its formatting. Also, you may not want some of them to edit the document. Before sending the document for review, you can limit the ability to format and edit the document for specific users. This way you can prevent them from trying to modify the contents or determining how something is formatted, and keep them focused on the task at hand. It also ensures that you won't have to undo any formatting changes they might have made.

The Restrict Formatting and Editing Task Pane

The **Restrict Formatting and Editing** task pane is used to apply formatting and editing restrictions to a document. It consists of three sections.

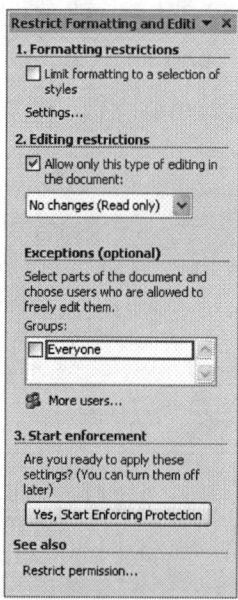

Figure 6-1: Options available in the Restrict Formatting and Editing task pane.

Section	Description
Formatting restrictions	Limits formatting to the set of styles specified in the **Formatting Restrictions** dialog box.
Editing restrictions	Restricts the type of editing that can be performed in a document.
Start enforcement	Enforces the restrictions specified in the **Restrict Formatting and Editing** task pane.

Editing Restrictions

There are four types of editing restrictions that can be enforced on a document.

Type	Description
Tracked changes	Forces change tracking to be enabled.
Comments	Allows only comments to be added to the protected document.
Filling in forms	Allows only information to be entered in form fields.
No changes (Read only)	Prevents any changes from being made to the document.

Protected View

The **Protected View** is a read-only view, which is enabled by default whenever a Word document is downloaded from the Internet. To edit the document, you have to click **Enable Editing** in the message bar. Since this feature does not allow editing, you may want to turn off the protected view by disabling the **Enable Protected View for files originating from the Internet** option in the **Protected View** category of the **Trust Center** dialog box.

How to Set Formatting and Editing Restrictions

Procedure Reference: Limit Formatting Choices in a Document

To limit formatting choices in a document:

1. If necessary, add the developer tab to the Ribbon.

    a. In the **Word Options** dialog box, select the **Customize Ribbon** category.

    b. in the **Customize the Ribbon** section, check **Developer** and click **OK.**

2. Display the **Restrict Formatting and Editing** task pane.

    - Display the **Restrict Formatting and Editing** task pane using the Ribbon.

        a. On the **Developer** tab, in the **Protect** group, click **Restrict Editing.**

        b. Or, on the **Review** tab, in the **Protect** group, click **Restrict Editing.**

    - Or, display the **Restrict Formatting and Editing** task pane using the Back Stage mode.

        a. Select the **File** tab.

        b. In the **Permissions** section, click **Protect Document** and choose **Restrict Editing.**

    - Or, display the **Restrict Formatting and Editing** task pane using the **Save As** dialog box.

        a. On the **File** tab, choose **Save As.**

        b. In the **Save As** dialog box, click **Tools** and choose **General Options.**

        c. In the **General Options** dialog box, click **Protect Document.**

        d. Close the **Save As** dialog box.

3. If you previously enforced any type of protection on the document, click **Stop Protection,** and in the **Unprotect Document** dialog box, enter the password that you entered for protecting the document at that time, and click **OK.**

4. In the **Formatting restrictions** section, check **Limit formatting to a selection of styles.**

5. Click **Settings.**

6. In the **Checked styles are currently allowed** list box, uncheck the styles you want to prevent from being used and click **OK.**

7. In the **Microsoft Word** message box, click **Yes.**

8. In the **Restrict Formatting and Editing** task pane, in the **Start enforcement** section, click **Yes, Start Enforcing Protection.**

9. In the **Start Enforcing Protection** dialog box, enter and re-enter the password to enforce the formatting restriction and click **OK.**

Procedure Reference: Specify Editing Restrictions for a Document

To specify editing restrictions for a document:

1. Display the **Restrict Formatting and Editing** task pane.

2. If you previously enforced any type of protection on the document, click **Stop Protection,** in the **Unprotect Document** dialog box, enter the password that you entered for protecting the document, and click **OK.**

3. In the **Editing restrictions** section, check **Allow only this type of editing in the document.**

4. From the **Editing Restrictions** drop-down list, select the desired type of editing to allow.

5. If necessary, in the **Exceptions (optional)** section, add new user groups to provide access to a particular group of users.

    a. Click **More Users.**

    b. In the **Add Users** dialog box, in the **Enter user names, separated by semicolons** text box, type the usernames to be added, separated by semicolons.

    c. Click **OK.**

6. Select the content for which the editing restriction is to be applied.

7. If necessary, in the **Groups** list box, check the desired group to apply the editing restriction.

8. If necessary, in the **Individuals** list box, check the desired individuals to apply the editing restriction.

 When you select more than one individual, the individuals are grouped and listed in the **Groups** list box.

9. In the **Start enforcement** section, click **Yes, Start Enforcing Protection.**

10. In the **Start Enforcing Protection** dialog box, enter and re-enter a password and click **OK.**

11. If necessary, click **Find Next Region I Can Edit** to navigate to the next region that can be edited.

12. If necessary, click **Show All Regions I Can Edit** to highlight all regions that can be edited.

13. If necessary, click in a region that can be edited and apply editing restrictions to it.

Procedure Reference: Remove Formatting and Editing Restrictions

To remove formatting or editing restrictions:

1. In the **Restrict Formatting and Editing** task pane, click **Stop Protection.**

2. If necessary, in the **Unprotect Document** dialog box, in the **Password** text box, type the password and click **OK.**

3. In the **Editing Restrictions** section, uncheck **Allow only this type of editing in the document** and click **Yes** to remove the ignored exceptions.

4. Uncheck **Limit formatting to a selection of styles** and close the task pane.

ACTIVITY 6-3
Setting Formatting and Editing Restrictions

Data Files:

C:\084584Data\Securing a Document\Financial Highlights.docx

Before You Begin

In the **Word Options** dialog box, select the **Customize Ribbon** tab, and in the **Customize the Ribbon** section, check **Developer** and click **OK** to add the **Developer** tab to the Ribbon.

Scenario:

You want your colleagues to provide their comments on the financial highlights. However, you don't want them to modify the contents.

---

1. Apply editing restrictions to the document.

   a. From the C:\084584Data\Securing a Document folder, open the Financial Highlights.docx file.

   b. On the **Developer** tab, in the **Protect** group, click **Restrict Editing**.

   c. In the **Restrict Formatting and Editing** task pane, in the **Editing restrictions** section, check **Allow only this type of editing in the document.**

   d. In the **Editing restrictions** drop-down list, verify that **No changes (Read only)** is selected.

---

2. Enforce the editing restrictions.

   a. In the **Start enforcement** section, click **Yes, Start Enforcing Protection.**

   b. In the **Start Enforcing Protection** dialog box, in the **Password** section, in the **Enter new password (optional)** text box, type *p@ssw0rd*

   c. In the **Reenter password to confirm** text box, type *p@ssw0rd* and click **OK.**

   d. In the **Restrict Formatting and Editing** task pane, in the **Your Permissions** section, notice the message indicating that the document is protected from unintentional editing. Close the **Restrict Formatting and Editing** task pane.

   e. Save the document as *My Financial Highlights*

---

3. Test the restrictions imposed on the document.

   a. Select any text in the document and press **Delete.**

   b. Notice that you are not able to delete the selected text. Close the document.

TOPIC D
Add a Digital Signature to a Document

You now know how to prevent formatting and editing changes to your document. Another security concern is verifying the source of a document and checking whether it contains the original contents. In this topic, you will add a digital signature to a document.

If a document is electronically signed, then it is a valid document. Changes in a digital signature can be detected electronically, helping ensure that the document is free from forgery and false information. Also, the author cannot deny the fact that he created and sent the document. Word 2010 locks documents that are digitally signed, and any attempt to tamper with the documents will make the signature invalid.

Digital Certificates

A *digital certificate* is an electronic file that contains unique information about a specific person. It contains a serial number, a digital signature from a certificate-issuing authority, expiration dates, a name, and a copy of the certificate holder's public key so that a recipient can verify that the certificate is authentic. It is issued by a certification authority *(CA)*, which is a trusted third party, or from your company's computer department. If you do not want to purchase digital certificates issued by a third party, you can create your own digital ID but other people cannot verify the authenticity of the signature. A digital certificate is also known as a digital ID because it is used to digitally sign a document.

Digital Signature

Definition:

A *digital signature* is a content authentication tool that authenticates the sender of a file and ensures the integrity of digital documents. When you attach a digital signature to a document, the document is considered to be signed. Once signed, the document cannot be modified without removing the digital signature. The signature can be both visible and invisible.

Example:

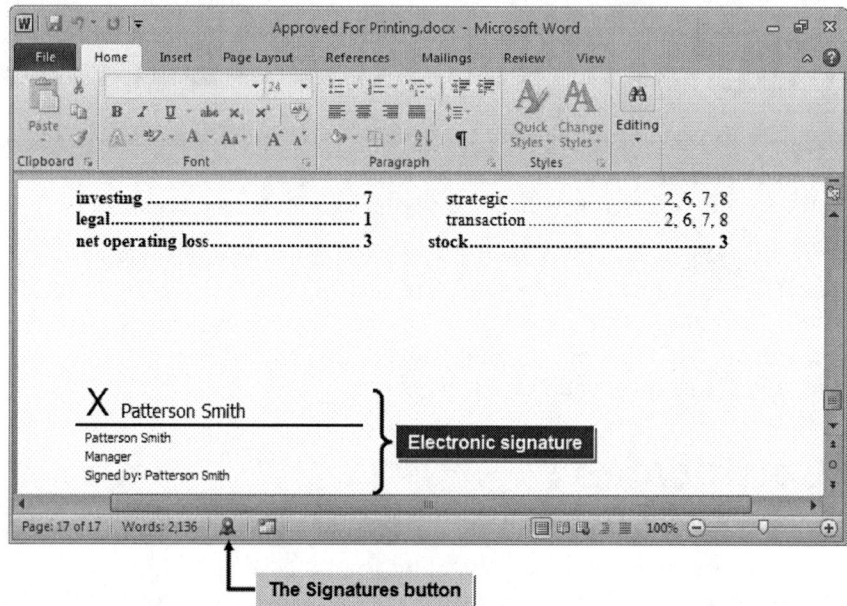

Figure 6-2: A document with an electronic signature.

The Signature Line

A *signature line* is used to add a digital signature to a document. A signature line is usually found at the end of the document, though it can be used anywhere in the document. It records the contents exactly as it was when signed, and also allows the signature to be verified when needed. You can add either text or images to a signature line.

The Signatures Task Pane

The *Signatures task pane* lists all signatures in a document. It groups signatures based on either of these two categories: **Valid signatures** or **Requested signatures. Valid signatures** include all the information and signature details. The **Requested signatures** include only the signature setup information.

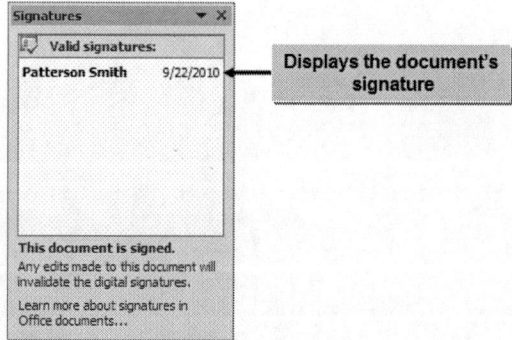

Figure 6-3: The Signatures task pane lists the signatures in a document.

Requested Signatures

Requested signatures are signatures that contain the setup information required for creating a signature. This could include information such as the signer's name, title, email address, and other instructions for the signer. The digital certificate will not be issued until the signature becomes a valid one, which can be done by signing the document.

Valid Signatures

Valid signatures are signatures that contain signature details in addition to the signature setup information. In addition to the signer's name, title, email address and other instructions, **Valid signatures** also contain the text or image used to sign a document digitally. **Valid signatures** imply that there are no issues with the certificate.

How to Add a Digital Signature to a Document

Procedure Reference: Add a Signature Line

To add a signature line:

1. Display the **Signature Setup** dialog box.

   - On the **Insert** tab, in the **Text** group, click the **Signature Line** drop-down and choose **Microsoft Office Signature Line.**

   - Or, on the **File** tab, in the **Permissions** section, from the **Protect Document** drop-down, choose **Add a Digital Signature.**

2. In the **Microsoft Word** message box, click **OK** to specify signature settings.

3. In the **Signature Setup** dialog box, specify the desired options.

   a. In the **Suggested signer** text box, type a name.

   b. In the **Suggested signer's title** text box, type a designation.

   c. In the **Suggested signer's e-mail address** text box, type an email address.

   d. If necessary, in the **Instructions to the signer** text box, type the desired instructions.

   e. Check **Allow the signer to add comments in the Sign dialog** to allow comments to be added along with the signature.

   f. Check **Show sign date in signature line** to show the date when the signature is added in the signature line.

4. Click OK to add a signature line.

Procedure Reference: Sign a Document

To sign a document:

1. Double-click the signature line.

2. In the **Microsoft Word** message box, click **OK** to enter your signature.

3. If necessary, specify the details required to create your own digital ID.

   a. In the **Get a Digital ID** dialog box, select **Create your own digital ID** and click **OK.**

   b. In the **Create a Digital ID** dialog box, specify the necessary details and click **Create.**

4. In the **Sign** dialog box, specify the appropriate options.

   - In the **X** text box, type your name to add a printed version of your signature.

Tablet PC users can sign their names in the text box next to the X by using the inking feature to add a handwritten signature.

- Or, click **Select Image**, navigate to and select the desired image, and click **Select** to select an image of the written signature.

5. Click **Sign**, and in the **Signature Confirmation** dialog box, click **OK.**

6. If necessary, remove the digital signature.

    a. Display the **Signatures** task pane.

        - In the status bar, click the red ribbon icon.

        - Or, on the **File** tab, in the **Permissions** section, choose **Protect Document**→ **Add a Digital Signature.**

    b. Remove the signature.

        - In the **Valid Signatures** list box, select the signature, click the signature's drop-down arrow and choose **Remove Signature.**

        - Or, right-click the digital signature and choose **Remove Signature.**

    c. In the **Remove Signature** dialog box, click **Yes.**

    d. In the **Signature Removed** dialog box, click **OK.**

ACTIVITY 6-4
Adding a Digital Signature to a Document

Data Files:

C:\084584Data\Securing a Document\Approved For Printing.docx

Scenario:

Your commercial printer has notified you that another person in your company has been sending print jobs to them using your name. As a result, your department is being billed for unapproved work. You need to avoid the recurrence of such incidents.

---

1. Add a signature line.

    a. From the C:\084584Data\Securing a Document folder, open the Approved For Printing.docx file.

    b. Save the document as **My Approved For Printing**

    c. Place your cursor at the end of the document.

    d. On the **Insert** tab, in the **Text** group, click the **Signature Line** drop-down and choose **Microsoft Office Signature Line.**

    e. In the **Microsoft Word** message box, click **OK.**

    f. In the **Signature Setup** dialog box, in the **Suggested signer** text box, type **Mary Coleman**

    g. In the **Suggested signer's title** text box, type **Manager**

    h. In the **Suggested signer's e-mail address** text box, type **mcoleman@ourglobalcompany.com** and click **OK** to add a placeholder for the digital signature.

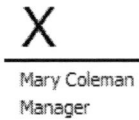

---

2. Sign the document.

    a. Double-click the digital ID placeholder and, in the **Microsoft Word** message box, click **OK.**

    b. In the **Get a Digital ID** dialog box, select **Create your own digital ID** and click **OK.**

    c. In the **Create a Digital ID** dialog box, in the **Name** text box, triple-click and type **Mary Coleman**

    d. In the **E-mail address** text box, type **mcoleman@ourglobalcompany.com**

    e. In the **Organization** text box, type **Our Global Company** and click **Create.**

---

f. In the **Sign** dialog box, in the **X** text box, type your name and click **Sign.**

g. In the **Signature Confirmation** dialog box, click **OK.**

h. Observe that the name you entered is displayed as the digital signature.

Mary Coleman
Manager
Signed by: Mary Coleman

3. Test the digital signature.

a. In the message bar, click **Edit Anyway.**

b. Observe that a **Microsoft Word** message box is displayed indicating that editing will remove the signatures in the document. Click **No** and close the document.

TOPIC E

Set a Password for a Document

So far, you have learned how to prevent information from being modified. You can also prevent unauthorized users from opening a document. In this topic, you will set a password for a document.

There are chances for you to mistakenly send documents with sensitive information in them. You can avoid such situations by password protecting your document. Password protected documents permit only an authorized user to make changes.

How to Set a Password for a Document

Procedure Reference: Set a Password for a Document

To set a password for a document:

1. Open the document you want to encrypt with a password.
   - Set the password using the Ribbon options.
     a. On the **File** tab, choose **Save As.**
     b. In the **Save As** dialog box, click **Tools** and choose **General Options.**
     c. In the **General Options** dialog box, in the **Password to open** text box, type a password of your choice and click **OK.**
     d. In the **Confirm Password** dialog box, in the **Reenter password to open** text box, retype the password and click **OK.**
   - Set the password using the Back Stage mode.
     a. On the **File** tab, in the **Permissions** section, click **Protect Document** and choose **Encrypt with Password.**
     b. In the **Encrypt Document** dialog box, in the **Password** text box, type a password of your choice and click **OK.**
     c. In the **Confirm Password** dialog box, in the **Reenter password** text box, enter the same password and click **OK.**

2. Save the document to set the password.

3. If necessary, verify that the document has been password protected.
   a. Close the password-protected document.
   b. Reopen the password-protected document.
   c. In the **Password** dialog box, in the **Enter password to open file** text box, type the correct password.
   d. Click **OK** to open the document.

4. If desired, remove the password.
   a. Display the **Save As** dialog box, and from the **Tools** drop-down, choose **General Options.**
   b. In the **General Options** dialog box, in the **Password to open** text box, delete the password, and click **OK.**
   c. Save the document to remove the password.

Password Tips

Passwords protect your document from unintentional editing. Passwords are case sensitive and can include up to 15 letters, numbers, punctuation, spaces, and symbols. By mixing a variety of cases and characters, you can make the password difficult to guess. However, you also need to ensure that your password is memorable because if you forget it, you will have difficulties opening the document.

ACTIVITY 6-5
Setting a Password for a Document

Data Files:

C:\084584Data\Securing a Document\Salary Review.docx

Scenario:

The Salary Review document contains sensitive information on certain employees who can be approved for a raise. You want to make sure that only authorized people are able to open the document.

---

1. Password protect the document.

   a. From the C:\084584Data\Securing a Document folder, open the Salary Review.docx file.

   b. Select the **File** tab, and in the Backstage view, in the **Permissions** section, click the **Protect Document** drop-down and choose **Encrypt with Password.**

   c. In the **Encrypt Document** dialog box, in the **Password** text box, type *p@ssw0rd* and click **OK.**

   d. In the **Confirm Password** dialog box, in the **Reenter password** text box, type *p@ssw0rd* and click **OK.**

   e. Save the document as *My Salary Review* and close it.

---

2. Verify that the document is password protected.

   a. Select the **File** tab, and in the Backstage view, from the **Recent Documents** section, open the My Salary Review.docx file.

   b. In the **Password** dialog box, in the **Enter password to open file** text box, type *p@ssw0rd* and click **OK.**

   c. Observe that My Salary Review.docx opens.

   d. Close My Salary Review.docx.

TOPIC F

Restrict Document Access

In the previous topic, you learned how to password protect a document. Applying levels of permission is another way to control access to your documents. In this topic, you will restrict access to a document.

In the course of your work, you may need to prevent sensitive information from being reused in any form, be it hard copy or electronic. By setting varying levels of permission, you can restrict the usage of the contents in a document.

Information Rights Management

Information Rights Management (IRM) is a service that permits users and administrators to define the access permission for presentations, documents, workbooks, and other Office suite applications such as Outlook and Microsoft Access. The permissions assigned to a file are stored with the file's contents. All data present within a document is bound by these permissions. The IRM also enables you to prohibit the printing, forwarding, or copying of sensitive data. The contents also cannot be copied using the Print Screen mode of Windows. In addition, you can set an expiration date to restrict file access after a specific time frame. IRM is otherwise known as Digital Rights Management (DRM).

Windows Rights Management Services Client with Service Pack 2

If you are using Windows XP as the operating system for your computer, then you need to install Windows Rights Management Services Client with Service Pack 2, which is the IRM administrator. The Rights Management account certificate becomes available on your system upon installation of the Windows Rights Management Services Client with Service Pack 2. Organization-specific policies on copying, forwarding, and editing can be configured using the server. If you are using Windows Vista, the Windows Rights Management Services Client is configured by default during the installation of the operating system.

The Rights Management Account Certificate

For those who are not using the IRM administrator, there is an option for using your email address and password configured on .NET Passport, MSN, Hotmail, or Windows Live. Your email address is used to create the Rights Management account certificate that is downloaded to your computer. You can choose to download a standard certificate or a temporary certificate, depending on the use. Once the Rights Management account certificate is downloaded, you can create user accounts, which is the addition of the email address of the persons to whom you will send your document. You can give users full control over your document or restrict them to read, print, or copy.

Standard and Temporary Certificates

You can choose to download a standard certificate or a temporary certificate when you are using your email address and password to download the Rights Management account certificate. If you are going to use the contents in the document for a limited time, or if you are using a public computer to send your document, then the temporary certificate will suffice. Downloading the standard certificate enables you to create, use, and view restricted content on your PC. The certificate can also be renewed on its expiration.

Access Levels

Access levels determine the permission granted to a user to manipulate the contents of a document.

Level	Description
Read	Allows the user read-only access to a document.
Change	Allows the user to read, edit, and save changes to a document.
Full Control	Allows the user to read, edit, save changes, and print a document.

The Mark As Final Option

The **Mark as Final** option can be used to inform users that the document received by them is the final version. When you set the **Mark as Final** option for a document, the document is saved in the read-only mode. When a reader opens the document in Word, all editing tools are disabled and the **Marked as Final** icon is displayed on the status bar. A reader can change the status and edit the document by deselecting the **Mark as Final** option.

 When you open a document that is marked as final in earlier versions of Word, it does not open in the read-only mode. All editing tools will be accessible.

How to Restrict Document Access

Procedure Reference: Restrict Access to Content in a Document

To restrict access to the contents of a document using IRM:

1. On the **File** tab, in the **Permissions** section, click **Protect Document** and choose **Restrict Permission by People→Restricted Access.**

2. In the **Permission** dialog box, check the **Restrict permission to this document** check box.

 To display the Permission dialog box, you need to configure Information Rights Management in Office 2010 running on XP. Users can restrict permission to documents using IRM.

3. In the **Choose Profile** dialog box, click **OK.**

4. In the **Read** or **Change** text box, enter the email addresses of specific users, as desired.

5. Click **More Options** and, in the **The following users have permission to this document** list box, select the desired user.

6. From the **Access Level** drop-down list for that user, select the desired access level.

7. If necessary, set an expiration date for a document.

    a. In the **Additional permissions for users** section, check **This document expires on.**

    b. Click the **This document expires on** drop-down arrow, and using the date picker, select a date.

8.   Click **OK** to exit the **Permission** dialog box.

Procedure Reference: Mark a Document as Final

To mark a document as final:

1.   On the File tab, in the **Permissions** section, click **Protect Document** and choose **Mark as Final.**

2.   In the warning box that indicates that the document will be marked as final and saved, click **OK.**

3.   In the message box that indicates that the document has been marked as final, click **OK.**

ACTIVITY 6-6
Restricting Document Access

Data Files:

C:\084584Data\Securing a Document\Strategy Text.docx

Before You Begin

1. Ensure that Windows Rights Management Services is installed.

2. You need a Windows Live or Hotmail ID.

Scenario:

You are to mail a document that contains vital information about your company's strategies. And with security being a major concern, you decide to assign permission levels to restrict unauthorized users from accessing the document. You also need to make sure that the document is not accessed after a specific time by any user.

---

1. Restrict permission to the Strategy document.

   a. From the C:\084584Data\Securing a Document folder, open the Strategy Text.docx file.

   b. Save the document as *My Strategy Text*

   c. Select the **File** tab, and in the Backstage view, in the **Permissions** section, click the **Protect Document** drop-down and choose **Restrict Permission by People**→ **Restricted Access.**

   d. In the **Select User** dialog box, click **OK.**

   e. In the **Permission** dialog box, check **Restrict permission to this document**

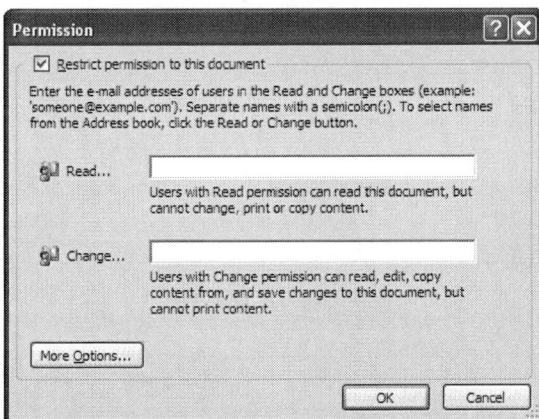

   f. In the **Read** text box, type *mcoleman@ourglobalcompany.com* and click **More Options.**

     g.   In the **The following users have permission to this document** list box, verify that Access Level for **mcoleman@ourglobalcompany.com** is **Read.**

2.   Set an expiration date for the document.

     a.   In the **Additional permissions for users** section, check **This document expires on.**

     b.   Click the **This document expires on** drop-down arrow and specify an expiry date for the document.

     c.   Click **OK** to close the **Permission** dialog box.

     d.   Observe that a message is displayed in the **Permissions** section, indicating that access to the document has been restricted to certain people.

3.   Mark the document as final.

     a.   Click **Protect Document** and choose **Mark as Final.**

     b.   In the **Microsoft Word** message box, click **OK.**

     c.   Notice that a message indicating that the document has been marked as final is displayed in the **Permissions** section.

     d.   Close the document.

Lesson 6 Follow-up

In this lesson, you improved the security of a document by updating its properties with accurate personal information and by setting formatting and editing restrictions. You then added a digital signature and a password to the document. You can use one or more of these security methods in order to secure your own documents.

1. **What security measures do you currently use to protect your documents?**

2. **How do you build a strong password to protect your documents?**

7 | Creating Forms

Lesson Time: 45 minutes

Lesson Objectives:

In this lesson, you will create forms.

You will:

- Add form fields to a document.
- Protect a form.
- Automate a form.

Introduction

During the course of a workday, you may need to collect some information from customers or coworkers. In this lesson, you will create forms so that you can collect the desired information in a consistent and efficient manner.

Every day you may get dozens of phone calls from people wanting to be added to your company's mailing list. You may need to obtain the same information from each person. Using Word, you can create forms to help you consistently capture standard information.

TOPIC A
Add Form Fields to a Document

In this lesson, you will create forms to use in Word. The first step to using any form is setting up the fields and layout of the form. In this topic, you will add form fields to a document.

When you are collecting a standard set of information from a large group of people, trying to question them from memory and noting down the details in a document might lead to inconsistencies or missing out on some important details. When you have a form containing fields for you to enter all of those necessary details, it helps if you ask for the required information and capture it in an organized format.

Forms

Definition:

A *form* is a document used for collecting information in a consistent format. Both paper-based and electronic forms contain boilerplate text such as the form title, labels, and fields. Users can enter information in these fields, but they will not be able to alter the form.

Example:

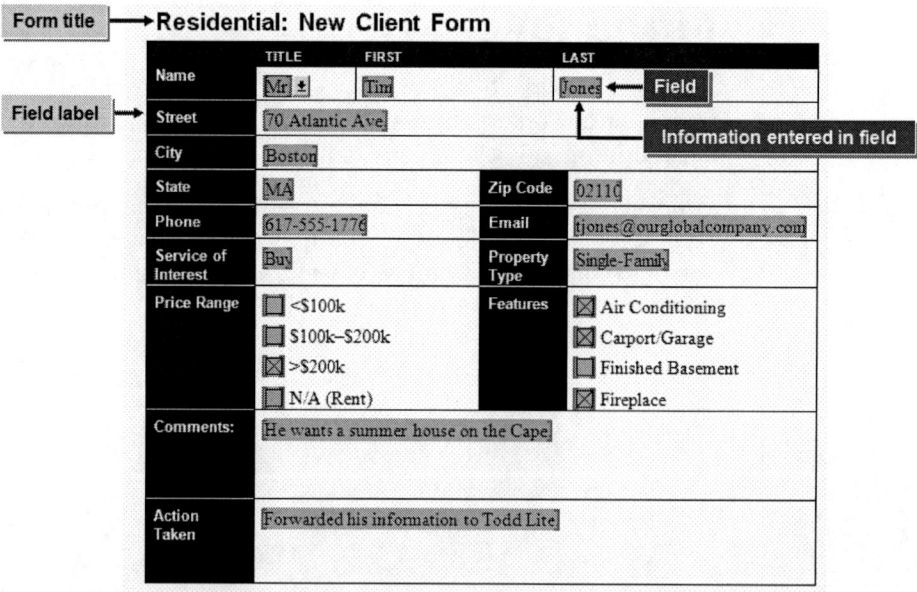

Figure 7-1: A sample form with client information.

Plan a Form

Before you begin creating a form in Word, you should decide what information you want to capture and where you want that information to appear in the form. You also need to consider how the form will be distributed and whether or not you want to protect the form. When you begin creating the form, consider using a table to contain the various form fields. Tables allow you to control the form's layout with more precision.

Using an existing paper form or diagramming a new form on paper is a useful way to plan a form. By experimenting with paper diagrams, you can save time when you start inserting form fields.

Form Fields

Definition:

A *form field* is a container inserted into a form used for collecting a specific type of information. Each form field has a name signifying the type of entry it requires. Form fields also have their own set of options. These options can be used to determine the type and format of data that a user is allowed to enter and how the input is captured.

Example:

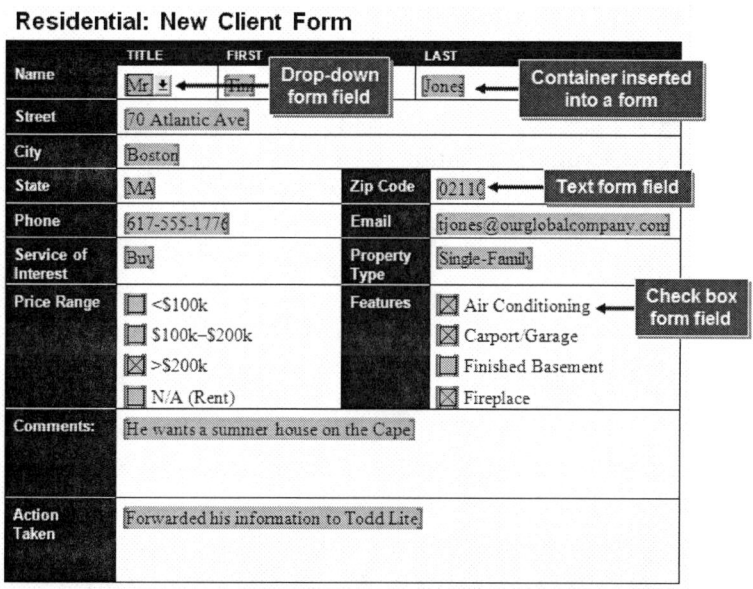

Figure 7-2: A form field allows you to collect a specific type of information.

Types of Form Fields

Each form field can be used to collect a particular type of data. There are three types of form fields.

Form Field	Description
Text	Used to collect textual, numeric, or date-related information.
Check Box	Used to allow users to select several answers from several choices.
Drop-Down	Used to allow users to select a single answer from several choices.

Form Field Options

The form field options vary based on the type of form field selected.

Form Field	Options Include
Text	Type of data that can be entered; default text to be displayed; maximum field length; text, number, and date formats; macro handling; bookmark names; and help text options.
Check Box	Check box size; default value; macro handling; bookmark names; and help text options.
Drop-Down	Drop-down items; item order; macro handling; bookmark names; and help text options.

Legacy Tools

Legacy Tools contains options to add form fields and ActiveX controls to a document. It can be accessed on the **Developer** tab in the **Controls** group.

The Controls Group

The **Controls** group contains content controls and form fields, which you can use to design forms. It also contains the **Properties** button, which is used to display the properties of a form field or a content control.

ActiveX Controls

ActiveX Controls are software components that can be used to perform specific tasks. You can run **ActiveX Controls** from within the Word application. **ActiveX Controls** have access to the complete Windows operating system.

Content Controls

Content controls are controls that can be added to forms, templates, and documents. They can be designed to collect a specific type of information.

How to Add Form Fields to a Document

Procedure Reference: Add a Drop-Down Form Field

To add a drop-down form field:

1. If necessary, display the **Developer** tab on the Ribbon.
   a. Display the **Word Options** dialog box.
   b. In the left pane, select **Customize Ribbon.**
   c. In the right pane, in the **Customize the Ribbon** section, in the **Main Tabs** subsection, check **Developer** and click **OK.**
2. Place the insertion point where you want to insert the drop-down form field.
3. On the **Developer** tab, in the **Controls** group, click **Legacy Tools** and then, in the **Legacy Forms** section, select **Drop-Down Form Field.**
4. In the **Controls** group, click **Properties.**

5. In the **Drop-Down Form Field Options** dialog box, set the drop-down form field's options.

    a. In the **Drop-down item** text box, type the name of a list item.

    b. Click **Add** to add the item to the list.

    c. If necessary, add more list items.

    d. If necessary, select a list item and click the appropriate button to move the item up or down until the item is in the desired position.

    e. If necessary, select an item and click **Remove** to remove the item.

6. Click **OK** to insert the drop-down form field.

 To display a field's properties, double-click or right-click the form field and choose **Properties.**

 After you create a form field, you will need to protect the form for the fields to work as intended.

Procedure Reference: Add a Text Form Field

To add a text form field:

1. Place the insertion point where you want to insert the text form field.

2. On the **Developer** tab, in the **Controls** group, click **Legacy Tools** and then, in the **Legacy Forms** section, select **Text Form Field.**

3. Click **Properties.**

4. If necessary, in the **Text Form Field Options** dialog box, set the text form field's options.

    a. From the **Type** drop-down list, select the type of information that will be entered in the form field.

        ●   **Regular text**: Use when the form field will contain basic text.

        ●   **Number**: Use when the form field will contain numbers that you want formatted in a particular way.

        ●   **Date**: Use when the form field will contain a date.

        ●   **Current date**: Use when the form field should contain the current date.

        ●   **Current time**: Use when the form field should contain the current time.

        ●   **Calculation**: Use when the form field should contain a mathematical calculation.

    b. In the **Default text** text box, type the default information that will be initially displayed in the form field.

 Depending on the type you select, the **Default text** text box may also display the default number, default date, or default expression.

    c.   In the **Maximum length** spin box, set the desired number of characters that can be entered in the form field.

    d.   From the **Text format** drop-down list, select the desired format.

 Depending on the type you select, the **Text format** drop-down list may also display the **Number format**, **Date format**, or **Time format** option.

5.   Click **OK** to insert the text form field.

Procedure Reference: Add a Check Box Form Field

To add a check box form field:

1.   Place the insertion point where you want to insert the check box form field.

2.   On the **Developer** tab, in the **Controls** group, click **Legacy Tools** and then, in the **Legacy Forms** section, select **Check Box Form Field** to insert the check box form field.

3.   Click **Properties.**

4.   If necessary, in the **Check Box Form Field Options** dialog box, set the check box form field options.

    a.   Set the size of the check box.

- Set the check box size to **Auto.**
- Or, set the check box size to an exact size by specifying points in the **Exactly** spin box.

    b.   Set the default value of the check box.

- In the **Default value** section, select the **Not checked** option to set the default value of the check box as unchecked.
- Or, in the **Default value** section, select the **Checked** option to set the default value of the check box as checked.

5.   Click **OK** to insert the check box form field.

6.   Press the **Spacebar** and type the text that will act as the label for the check box.

Procedure Reference: Remove Fields from a Form

To remove fields from a form:

1.   Select the field you want to remove.

2.   Use the keyboard to remove the field.

- Press **Delete.**
- Press **Backspace.**

Form Field Shading Button

The **Form Field Shading** button is used to give a shading effect to the form field. It makes the field visible to the person developing the form.

ACTIVITY 7-1
Adding Form Fields to a Document

Data Files:

C:\084584Data\Creating Forms\New Client Form.docx

Scenario:

You have been asked to contribute to a new form that will eventually be a template used by OGC Properties customer service representatives to capture information from new clients interested in the company's residential services.

---

1. Insert a drop-down form field that lists all Title items.

    a. From the C:\084584Data\Creating Forms folder, open the New Client Form.docx file.

    b. In the form, in the table cell below **Title**, place the insertion point.

    c. On the **Developer** tab, in the **Controls** group, click the **Legacy Tools** drop-down, and then in the **Legacy Forms** section, select **Drop-Down Form Field.**

    d. In the **Controls** group, click **Properties.**

    e. In the **Drop-Down Form Field Options** dialog box, in the **Drop-down item** text box, type *Dr.* and click **Add.**

    f. Similarly, add *Miss, Mr., Mrs., Ms.,* and *Select One* as list items.

    g. Click the **Move** down arrow to move the **Select One** item to the top of the drop-down list and click **OK.**

    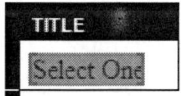

---

2. Insert text form fields for the client's first and last names.

    a. In the empty table cell below **First**, place the insertion point.

    b. In the **Controls** group, click the **Legacy Tools** drop-down and select **Text Form Field.**

    c. In the **Controls** group, click **Properties.**

    d. In the **Text Form Field Options** dialog box, in the **Default text** text box, type *First Name*

e.   From the **Text format** drop-down list, select **Title case** and click **OK.**

f.   In the empty cell below **Last**, insert a text form field.

g.   In the **Text Form Field Options** dialog box, enter the default text as ***Last Name***

h.   From the **Text format** drop-down list, select **Title case** and click **OK.**

3.   Insert a text form field for the zip code.

a.   In the empty cell to the right of the **Zip Code**, place the insertion point.

b.   Insert a text form field and display the **Text Form Field Options** dialog box.

c.   In the **Text form field** section, from the **Type** drop-down list, select **Number.**

d.   In the **Maximum length** spin box, triple-click and type *5*

e.   In the **Number format** text box, type *#####* and click **OK.**

 Each # represents a number.

4.   Insert check box form fields for the price range.

a.   In the empty cell to the right of **Price Range**, place the insertion point.

b.   In the **Controls** group, click the **Legacy Tools** drop-down and, in the **Legacy Forms** section, select **Check Box Form Field.**

c.   Press the **Spacebar**, type *<$100k* and press **Enter.**

d.   Insert a second check box form field with the label *$100k-$200k* and press **Enter.**

e.   Insert another two check box form fields with the labels *>$200k* and *N/A (Rent)*

5.   Insert text form fields for the client's contact information, comments, and actions taken.

a.   In the empty table cell to the right of **Street**, insert a text form field with the default text ***Street Name***

b.   In the empty table cell to the right of **City**, insert a text form field with the label ***City Name***

c.   In the empty table cell to the right of **Phone**, insert a text form field for the **Phone** field so that it accepts numbers in the format *###-###-####.*

d.   In the empty table cell to the right of **Email**, insert a text form field for the email address.

e.   In the empty table cell to the right of **Comments**, insert a text form field with the label ***Enter Comments Here*** and set the **Text format** property as **First Capital.**

f.   If necessary, scroll down, and in the empty table cell to the right of **Action Taken**, insert a text form field with the label ***Enter Actions Taken Here*** and set the **Text format** property as **First Capital.**

6.   Insert drop-down form fields containing list items for the **State, Service of Interest,** and **Property Type** fields.

a.   In the empty table cell to the right of **State**, insert a drop-down form field with the following items: ***Select One CA FL LA KY MA MD OH*** and ***TX***

b.   In the empty table cell to the right of **Service Of Interest**, insert a drop-down form field with the following items: ***Select One, Buy, Rent/Sublet,*** and ***Sell***

c.   In the empty table cell to the right of **Property Type**, insert a drop-down form field with the following items: ***Select One, Apartment, Condo/Town House, Multi-Family,*** and ***Single-Family***

7.   Insert check box form fields for the **Features** field.

a.   In the empty table cell to the right of **Features**, insert a check box form field with the label ***Air Conditioning***

b.   Similarly, add the following check box form fields below the **Air Conditioning** check box: ***Carport/Garage, Finished Basement,*** and ***Fireplace***

c.   Save the document as ***My New Client Form***

d.   If necessary, in the **Microsoft Word** message box, click **Yes.**

TOPIC B

Protect a Form

You have added form fields to a document. Now, you may want to ensure that only the form fields can be filled in and that the form's other contents cannot be altered. You also want to save that information in another file format so that it can be used by other programs. In this topic, you will protect and save a form.

You may spend hours creating forms and mailing them to people. Sometimes people may modify a form to suit their needs. Protecting the form will prevent them from making changes. Also, saving just the form data in a file that can be imported directly into the database can save a significant amount of time while avoiding possible data entry errors.

How to Protect a Form

Procedure Reference: Password Protect a Completed Form

To password protect a completed form:

1. On the **Developer** tab, in the **Protect** group, click **Restrict Editing.**
2. In the **Restrict Formatting and Editing** task pane, in the **Editing restrictions** section, check **Allow only this type of editing in the document.**
3. Below the check box, from the drop-down list, select **Filling in forms.**
4. In the **Start Enforcement** section, click **Yes, Start Enforcing Protection.**
5. In the **Start Enforcing Protection** dialog box, in the **Enter new password (optional)** text box, type the desired password and press **Tab.**
6. In the **Reenter password to confirm** text box, retype the password and click **OK** to protect the form.
7. If necessary, remove password protection from the form.
   a. If necessary, display the **Restrict Formatting and Editing** task pane.
   b. Click **Stop Protection.**
   c. In the **Unprotect Document** dialog box, in the **Password** text box, type the password and click **OK** to unprotect the form.

Locked Forms

When a form is locked, only the **Form Field Shading** buttons are enabled. Additionally, only the form fields themselves can be modified. Boilerplate text, page setup, and other formatting options are unavailable.

Procedure Reference: Add Custom Help to a Text Form Field

To add custom help to a form field:

1. Select the desired form field.
2. In the **Controls** group, click **Properties.**
3. In the **Text Form Field Options** dialog box, click **Add Help Text.**
4. In the **Form Field Help Text** dialog box, on the **Status Bar** tab, click in the **Type your own** text box and type the desired text.
5. Click **OK** to add the custom help text to the text form field.

Using Additional Help Text

If you need to provide a longer description than can be displayed on the status bar, you can type a longer help description in the **Type Your Own** text box on the **Help Key (F1)** tab. Both the status bar and the Help key can be used together. To display the Help key text, select the appropriate form field and press **F1.**

Procedure Reference: Reset Form Fields

To reset form fields:

1. On the Ribbon, select the **Developer** tab.

2. In the **Controls** group, click the **Legacy Tools** button and then, in the **Legacy Forms** section, select **Reset Form Fields** to reset the form fields to the default information.

Procedure Reference: Save Form Data as Plain Text

To save form data as plain text:

1. Display the **Save As** dialog box.

2. Click **Tools** and choose **Save Options.**

3. In the **Word Options** dialog box, in the left pane, select **Advanced** to display the advanced options in the right pane.

4. In the **Preserve fidelity when sharing this document** section, check **Save form data as delimited text file** and click **OK.**

5. If necessary, in the **Save As** dialog box, in the **File Name** text box, rename the file.

6. Click **Save.**

7. In the **File Conversion** dialog box, observe that the form data is displayed in the **Preview** list box and then click **OK.**

8. If necessary, open the form data text file to verify that the data was saved as expected.

Form Data Conversion

When you save form data as plain text, you can generally understand the form field results as they correspond with the order of the form fields in the form itself. Typically, drop-down form fields and text form fields provide logical and understandable results. However, when a check box form field is saved as text, the form field's result is displayed as either "0" or "1". A "0" means that the check box was unchecked; a "1" means that the check box was checked.

ACTIVITY 7-2
Protecting a Form

Before You Begin:
My New Client Form.docx is open.

Scenario:
The new client form is nearly done. All that remains to be done is to password protect the form, test the form, and modify the form fields as needed. After testing the form, you want to make sure that the form is password protected before saving it as a template.

---

1. Password protect the form by restricting access to it.

    a. On the **Developer** tab, in the **Protect** group, click **Restrict Editing.**

    b. In the **Restrict Formatting and Editing** task pane, in the **Editing restrictions** section, check **Allow only this type of editing in the document.**

    c. Below the check box, from the **Editing restrictions** drop-down list, select **Filling in forms.**

    d. In the **Start enforcement** section, click **Yes, Start Enforcing Protection.**

    e. In the **Start Enforcing Protection** dialog box, in the **Enter new password (optional)** text box, type **p@ssw0rd** and press **Tab.**

    f. In the **Reenter password to confirm** text box, type **p@ssw0rd** and click **OK.**

---

2. Test the form by entering some sample information.

    a. In the form, from the **Title** drop-down list, select **Ms.** and press **Tab** to move to the next field.

    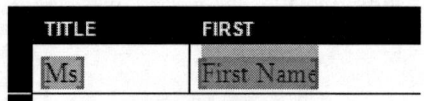

    b. Type **Sue** and press **Tab.**

    c. Type **Smith** and press **Tab.**

    d. Type **1 Elm Dr.** and press **Tab.**

    e. Type **Akron** and press **Tab.**

    f. From the **State** drop-down list, select **OH** and press **Tab.**

    g. In the **Zip Code** text field, type **44305** and press **Tab.**

    h. In the **Phone** text field, type **555-6560**

    i. Fill in the listed information in the appropriate form fields:
        - Email: *ssmith@ourglobalcompany.com*

- Service of Interest: *Buy*
- Property Type: *Single-Family*
- Price Range: *$100k–$200k*
- Features: *Air Conditioning, Carport/Garage*

3. Unprotect the form and add help text for the area code.

   a. In the **Restrict Formatting and Editing** task pane, click **Stop Protection.**

   b. In the **Unprotect Document** dialog box, in the **Password** text box, type *p@ssw0rd* and click **OK.**

   c. Next to the **Phone** label, double-click the text form field to display its properties.

   d. In the **Text Form Field Options** dialog box, click **Add Help Text.**

   e. In the **Form Field Help Text** dialog box, on the **Status Bar** tab, click in the **Type your own** text area, and type *Include the area code.* Click **OK.**

   f. In the **Text Form Field Options** dialog box, click **OK.**

4. Protect the form and test whether the help text works for Phone form field.

   a. In the **Restrict Formatting and Editing** task pane, in the **Start enforcement** section, click **Yes, Start Enforcing Protection.**

   b. In the **Start Enforcing Protection** dialog box, in the **Enter new password (optional)** text box, type *p@ssw0rd* and press **Tab.**

   c. In the **Reenter password to confirm** text box, type *p@ssw0rd* and click **OK.**

   d. Press **Tab** to deselect the **Phone** text form field.

   e. Select the **Phone** text form field.

   f. Observe that the help text is displayed in the status bar.

   > Include the area code.

   g. In the **Phone** text form field, type *330-555-6560*

5. Save the form as a template.

   a. Unprotect the form.

   b. In the **Controls** group, click the **Legacy Tools** button, and then in the **Legacy Forms** section, select **Reset Form Fields** [icon] to reset the form fields.

   c. Password protect the form.

   d. Display the **Save As** dialog box.

   e. From the **Save as type** drop-down list, select **Word Template (*.dotx).**

   f. In the **File name** text box, triple-click to select the existing text, type *My Protected New Client Form* and click **Save.**

   g. Close the template.

ACTIVITY 7-3
Saving Form Data as Plain Text

Data Files:

C:\084584Data\Creating Forms\Jones Client Form.docx

Scenario:

The company's technology department is experimenting with a new client database that requires information to be saved as text files. The technology department representative wants you to supply him with data from a sample client form that he can use in his testing.

---

1. Save the data in a form as a plain text file.

   a. From the C:\084584Data\Creating Forms folder, open the Jones Client Form.docx file.

   b. Display the **Save As** dialog box.

   c. Click **Tools** and choose **Save Options.**

   d. In the **Word Options** dialog box, in the left pane, select **Advanced** and scroll down to the **Preserve fidelity when sharing this document** section.

   e. Check **Save form data as delimited text file** and click **OK.**

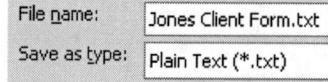

   f. In the **File name** text box, select "Jones Client Form.txt," type ***My Database Sample*** and click **Save.**

   g. Notice that, in the **File Conversion - My Database Sample.txt** dialog box, the form data is displayed in the **Preview** list box. Click **OK** to save the form data as a text file.

   h. Close the Jones Client Form.docx document without saving changes.

---

2. Open the plain text file.

   a. Display the **Open** dialog box.

   b. From the **Files of type** drop-down list, scroll down and select **Text Files (.txt).**

   c. Double-click **My Database Sample.txt** to view the form data.

   d. Close the My Database Sample.txt document.

TOPIC C
Automate a Form

You have saved the data entered in a form's fields as a text file. Forms don't always have to be static data containers. You can automate forms to accomplish a variety of tasks. In this topic, you will automate a form.

Adding the same information manually across a long document would require a lot of time. But, in Word, just entering the necessary information in the form will automatically update the information throughout the document. Also, using forms you can automate any task such as printing, formatting, and editing documents by adding appropriate form fields.

Form Field Settings

When a form field is created, it is given a generic bookmark name that describes the type of form field as well as the sequence in which the field was added to the form. For instance, the bookmark name "Dropdown4" identifies the fourth drop-down form field. Because a form field contains a bookmark name, the field's results can be cross-referenced. Because a form may contain dozens of similar fields, it is helpful to rename the bookmark so that it will be easier to locate or cross-reference. Additionally, you can check the **Calculate on exit** option if you plan on cross-referencing the form field. With this option checked, the cross-reference will be updated automatically when the user exits the form field.

 Remember, placing the mouse pointer over a cross-reference will display the name of the reference in a ScreenTip.

How to Automate a Form

Procedure Reference: Cross-Reference a Bookmarked Form Field

To cross-reference a bookmarked form field:

1. Prepare form fields to be cross-referenced.
   a. If necessary, unprotect the form.
   b. Display the form field's options.
   c. In the **Field settings** section, in the **Bookmark** text box, type a logical bookmark name.
   d. Check **Calculate on exit** and click **OK** to update the field automatically when the user exits the field.
2. Place the insertion point where you want to insert the cross-reference.
3. On the **References** tab, in the **Captions** group, click **Cross-reference.**
4. In the **Cross-reference** dialog box, from the **Reference type** drop-down list, select **Bookmark.**
5. If necessary, from the **Insert reference to** drop-down list, select **Bookmark text.**
6. In the **For which bookmark** list box, select the desired bookmark and click **Insert.**
7. Close the **Cross-reference** dialog box.

Usage of Cross-Referencing

When a form field is cross-referenced, the field's results can be displayed elsewhere in the same document. This is especially useful when creating your own form letters.

Procedure Reference: Run a Macro from a Form Field

To run a macro from a form field:

1. Display the options for the form field on which you want to run a macro.
2. In the **Run macro on** section, from the **Entry** drop-down list, select the macro you want to run while entering the field.
3. If necessary, from the **Exit** drop-down list, select the macro you want to run while exiting the field and click **OK.**

 You can run different macros upon entering the field and exiting the field.

Procedure Reference: Print Only the Data From a Form

To print only the data from a form:

1. On the **File** tab, choose **Print** and click **Page Setup.**
2. In the **Page Setup** dialog box, on the **Paper** tab, click **Print Options.**
3. In the **Word Options** dialog box, in the left pane, select **Advanced.**
4. Scroll down and in the **When printing this document** section, check **Print only the data from a form** and click **OK.**
5. In the **Print** dialog box, click **OK** to print the form data.

 If your company uses preprinted forms, you can design your Word form so that the data from your Word form fills in the corresponding form field on the preprinted form.

ACTIVITY 7-4
Automating a Form

Data Files:

C:\084584Data\Creating Forms\Printable New Client Form.dotm

Before You Begin:

1. Enable macros.

   a. On the **File** tab, choose **Options.**

   b. In the **Word Options** dialog box, in the left pane, select **Trust Center.**

   c. In the right pane, click **Trust Center Settings.**

   d. In the **Trust Center** dialog box, in the right pane, in the **Macro Settings** section, select **Enable all macros (not recommended; potentially dangerous code can run)** and click **OK.**

   e. In the **Word Options** dialog box, click **OK.**

2. In the **Open** dialog box, change the file type to **All Files.**

3. Ensure that a physical printer is attached to the computer or a printer driver is installed.

Scenario:

Whenever a new client's information is taken, a form letter is printed and mailed to that client. The template for that form is nearly finished. You have been asked to automate the template so that the new client's name is automatically entered in the letter where appropriate. You also want to print the form letter and test the form once you have made all the changes, for which you use a macro.

---

1. Create a bookmark for the Title, First Name, and Last Name form fields.

   a. From the C:\084584Data\Creating Forms folder, open the Printable New Client Form.dotm file.

   b. In the form, in the cell below the word **TITLE**, double-click the drop-down form field.

   c. In the **Drop-Down Form Field Options** dialog box, in the **Field settings** section, in the **Bookmark** text box, triple-click and replace the default text with *Title*

   d. Check **Calculate on exit** and click **OK.**

   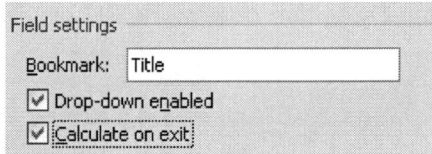

   e. In the cell below the word **FIRST**, double-click the text form field.

   f. In the **Text Form Field Options** dialog box, in the **Field settings** section, in the **Bookmark** text box, triple-click and replace the default text with *First*

g.   Check **Calculate on exit** and click **OK.**

h.   In the cell below the word **LAST**, double-click the text form field.

i.   In the **Text Form Field Options** dialog box, in the **Field settings** section, in the **Bookmark** text box, triple-click and replace the default text with *Last*

j.   Check **Calculate on exit** and click **OK.**

2.   Insert a cross-reference to the Title bookmark.

a.   Scroll down to the letter and, in the blank line above the **Street Name**, click to place the insertion point.

b.   On the **References** tab, in the **Captions** group, click **Cross-reference.**

c.   In the **Cross-reference** dialog box, from the **Reference type** drop-down list, select **Bookmark.**

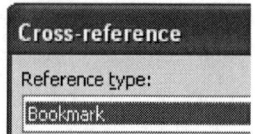

d.   Notice that **Bookmark text** is automatically selected in the **Insert reference to** drop-down list.

e.   In the **For which bookmark** list box, scroll down and select **Title.**

f.   Click **Insert** and then click **Close.**

3.   Insert cross-references to the First and Last bookmarks.

a.   Press the **Spacebar** and, in the **Captions** group, click **Cross-reference.**

b.   In the **Cross-reference** dialog box, in the **For which bookmark** list box, select **First** and click **Insert.**

c.   With the **Cross-reference** dialog box open, in the document, after the first name cross-reference, click to place the insertion point and press the **Spacebar.**

d.   In the **Cross-reference** dialog box, in the **For which bookmark** list box, select **Last** and click **Insert.**

e.   Click anywhere in the document.

f.   In the document, after the text "Dear" and before the colon, click to place the insertion point and press the **Spacebar.**

g.   In the **Cross-reference** dialog box, in the **For which bookmark** list box, select **First** and click **Insert.**

h.   Close the **Cross-reference** dialog box.

4.   Attach the Print Letter macro to the form.

a.   Scroll up the document to display the previous page.

b.   In the gray row at the end of the form, double-click the check box form field to display the **Check Box Form Field Options** dialog box.

c. In the **Run macro on** section, from the **Entry** drop-down list, select **Print_Letter** and click **OK.**

5. Test the form, including the print macro.

    a. Protect the form with the password *p@ssw0rd*

    b. Scroll up the document to view the top portion of the form.

    c. From the **Title** drop-down list, select **Mr.** and press **Tab** to move to the next field.

    d. Type *Miles* and press **Tab.**

    e. Type *Rodriguez*

    f. Fill in the listed information in the appropriate form fields:

    *   Street: *706 Branch Dr*
    *   City: *Boston*
    *   State: *MA*

    g. Scroll down and in the gray row at the end of the form, check the check box to print the letter.

    h. Scroll down to view the client details populated in the form letter.

     When the check box is checked, the print macro is triggered. You can see the form being printed in the status bar.

    i. Scroll up to the form and unprotect it.

    j. Reset the form.

    k. Protect the form with the password *p@ssw0rd*

    l. Save the file as *My Printable New Client Form* and close the document.

Lesson 7 Follow-up

In this lesson, you created forms. Forms provide an efficient way to collect required information from multiple sources.

1. **How do you decide on the features and requirements of a form?**

2. **What are the tasks you automate on your forms?**

Follow-up

In this course, you created, managed, revised, and distributed long documents and forms. Word provides advanced features that let you integrate it with other Office applications, and work in a collaborative mode.

1. How will you use other programs to enhance Word's functionality?

2. In Word, what collaboration tools will you use to manage documents?

3. What are the advantages of using Microsoft® Office SharePoint® Server 2010 as a document version control tool?

What's Next?

This course is the third and last in the series of Microsoft® Office Word 2010 courses. Following your Office Word training, you might want to take any one of a number of Element K courses focusing on various applications in the Microsoft Office 2010 suite such as *Microsoft® Office Excel® 2010* and *Microsoft® Office PowerPoint® 2010*.

A Office Word Mobile 2010

Microsoft Office Word Mobile 2010 lets you take Office applications with you wherever you go—whether you want to check an important document before a meeting or sign off a report that your team members are waiting for. Word Mobile enables you to open, view, and edit documents while you're on the move.

Word Mobile provides you with the same look and feel of the Word application that you're used to. It allows basic formatting of documents, and has the ability to save documents in multiple formats. You can insert pictures, lists, and tables in documents. The document formatting is preserved on your mobile device. In addition to the **Spell Check, AutoCorrect, Word Count,** and **Find and Replace** features, formatting commands such as bullets, numbering, fonts, and paragraph formats are also available. You can also email your documents from your mobile device or post them to your SharePoint site.

B | Create, Register, and Publish a Blog.

Blogs is a website or part of a website and allows users to post information over the Internet. Microsoft Office Word 2010 allows bloggers to publish their blogs easily and effectively to their blog accounts. A blog can be created by clicking the Blog Post from the Available templates section and inserting your own blog or by downloading a blog template from the office.com website. After you create a blog, it prompts you to register your blog account to any of the available blog providers. Choose your blog provider and enter your login information to log into your blog account. From the picture options dialog box, select your picture provider and publish your blog.

Creating a Blog Post:

1. Select the **File** tab, and from the **Available Templates** section, select **Blog Post**.

2. From the **Blog Post** section, click **Create**, to create a new blog post.

Register your Blog Account:

1. On the **Blog Post** tab, in the **Blog** group, select **Publish**.

2. In the **Register a Blog Account** dialog box, click **Register Now**.

3. In the **New Blog Account** dialog box, from the **Blog** drop-down menu, choose a service provider's name and click **Next**.

4. In the **service provider's account** dialog box, enter the necessary details to register the account.

5. Click **Picture Options**, and in the **Picture Options** dialog box, from the **Picture Provider** drop-down list, select the desired option and click **OK**.

Publish a Post:

1. On the **File** tab, choose **Save & Send**.

2. In the **Save & Send** section, click **Publish as Blog Post**.

3. Publish a Blog Post

    ●   On the **Blog Post** tab, in the **Blog** group, select **Publish**.

    ●   On the **Blog Post** tab, in the **Blog** group, select **Publish as draft**.

C | Microsoft Office Word 2010 Exam 77–881

Selected Element K courseware addresses Microsoft Office Specialist (MOS) certification skills for Microsoft Office 2010. The following table indicates where Word 2010 skills are covered. For example, 3-A indicates the lesson and topic number applicable to that skill, and 3-1 indicates the lesson and activity number.

Objective Domain	Level	Topic	Activity
1. Apply different views to a document.			
1.1 1 Select zoom options	1	1-C	1-3
1.1.2 Split windows	1	1-C	1-3
1.1.3 Arrange windows			
1.1.3.1 View Side by Side	1	1-C	1-3
1.1.3.2 Synchronous Scrolling	1	1-C	
1.1.4 Arrange document views			
1.1.4.1 Reorganize a document outline	3	1-B	
1.1.4.2 Master documents	3	5-F	5-8
1.1.4.3 Subdocuments	3	5-F	5-8
1.1.4.4 Web layout	1	1-C	
1.1.4.5 Draft	1	1-C	
1.1.5 Switch between windows	1	1-C	
1.1.6 Open a document in a new window	1	1-C	
1.2 Apply protection to a document.			
1.2.1 Apply protection by using the Microsoft Office Backstage view commands			
1.2.1.1 Apply controls and restrictions to document access	3	6-F	6-6
1.2.1.2 Password-protect a document	3	6-E	6-5
1.2.1.3 Mark as Final	3	6-F	6-6
1.2.2 Applying protection by using ribbon commands	3	6-F	
1.3 Manage document versions.			
1.3.1 Recover draft versions	1	1-E	

Objective Domain	Level	Topic	Activity
1.3.2 Delete all draft versions	1	1-E	
1.4 Share documents.			
1.4.1 Send documents via E-mail	3	1-C	
1.4.2 Send documents via SkyDrive	3	2-G	
1.4.3 Send documents via Internet fax	3	1-C	
1.4.4 Change file types	1	1-E	
1.4.5 Create PDF documents	1	1-E	
1.4.6 Create	3	Appendix A	
1.4.7 Publish a blog post	3	Appendix A	
1.4.8 Register a blog account	3	Appendix A	
1.5 Save a document.			
1.5.1 Use compatibility mode	1	1-E	
1.5.2 Use protected mode	3	6-C	6-3
1.5.3 Use Save As options	1	1-E	1-5
1.6 Apply a template to a document.			
1.6.1 Find templates			
1.6.1.1 Locate a template on your disk	2	8-A	
1.6.1.2 Find templates on the web	1	1-C	
2.1 Apply font and paragraph attributes.			
2.1.1 Apply character attributes	1	3-A	3-1
2.1.2 Apply styles	1	3-E	3-6
2.1.3 Use Format Painter	1	3-A	3-1
2.2 Navigate and search through a document.			
2.2.1 Use the Navigation Pane			
2.2.1.1 Headings	1	2-C	
2.2.1.2 Pages	1	2-C	
2.2.1.3 Results	1	2-C	
2.2.2 Use Go To	1	2-C	2-3
2.2.3 Use Browse by button	1	2-C	
2.2.4 Use Highlight features	1	3-A	3-2
2.2.5 Set Find and Replace options			
2.2.5.1 Format	1	3-F	
2.2.5.2 Special	1	2-C	
2.3 Apply indentation and tab settings to paragraphs.			
2.3.1 Apply indents			
2.3.1.1 first line	1	3-D	
2.3.1.2 hanging	1	3-D	
2.3.2 Sett tabs	1	3-B	3-3
2.3.3 Use the Tabs dialog box	1	3-B	

Objective Domain	Level	Topic	Activity
2.3.4 Set tabs on the ruler	1	3-B	3-5
2.3.5 Clear tab	1	3-B	
2.3.6 Set tab stops	1	3-B	3-5
2.3.7 Move tab stops	1	3-B	
2.4 Apply spacing settings to text and paragraphs.			
2.4.1 Set line spacing	1	3-D	3-5
2.4.2 Set paragraph spacing	1	3-D	3-5
2.5 Create tables.			
2.5.1 Use the Insert Table dialog box	1	5-A	5-1
2.5.2 Use Draw Table	1	5-A	
2.5.3 Insert a Quick Table	1	5-A	5-1
2.5.4 Convert text to table	1	5-D	5-4
2.5.5 Use a table to control page layout	1	5-A	
2.6 Manipulate tables in a document.			
2.6.1 Sort content	2	2-A	2-1
2.6.2 Add a row to a table	1	5-B	5-2
2.6.3 Add a column to a table	1	5-B	
2.6.4 Manipulate rows			
2.6.4.1 Split	1	5-B	
2.6.4.2 Merge	1	5-B	
2.6.4.3 Move	1	5-B	
2.6.4.4 Resize	1	5-B	
2.6.4.5 Delete	1	5-B	5-2
2.6.5 Manipulate columns			
2.6.5.1 Split	1	5-B	
2.6.5.2 Merge	1	5-B	
2.6.5.3 Move	1	5-B	5-2
2.6.5.4 Resize	1	5-B	5-2
2.6.5.5 Delete	1	5-B	
2.6.6 Define the header row	1	5-C	
2.6.7 Convert tables to text	1	5-D	5-4
2.6.8 View gridlines	1	5-B	
2.7 Apply bullets to a document.			
2.7.1 Apply bullets	1	3-C	
2.7.2 Select a symbol format	1	3-C	
2.7.3 Define a picture to be used as a bullet	2	1-C	
2.7.4 Use AutoFormat	1	3-C	
2.7.5 Promote and demote bullet levels	2	1-C	1-4
3.1 Apply and manipulate page setup settings.			

Objective Domain	Level	Topic	Activity
3.1.1 Set margins	1	3-D, 8-A	8-2
3.1.2 Insert non-breaking spaces	1	3-D	
3.1.3 Add hyphenation	1	3-D	
3.1.4 Add columns	2	7-C	7-3
3.1.5 Remove a break	1	8-A	
3.1.6 Force a page break	1	8-A	8-1
3.1.7 Insert a section break			
3.1.7.1 Continuous	2	7-B	7-2
3.1.7.2 Next page	2	7-B	
3.1.7.3 Next Odd	2	7-B	
3.1.7.4 Next Even	2	7-B	
3.1.8 Insert a blank page into a document	3	5-A	5-1
3.2 Apply themes.			
3.2.1 Use a theme to apply formatting	2	3-C	3-4
3.2.2 Customize a theme	2	3-C	3-4
3.3 Construct content in a document by using the Quick Parts tool.			
3.3.1 Add built-in building blocks			
3.3.1.1 Quotes	2	6-A	
3.3.1.2 Text boxes	2	6-A	6-1
3.3.1.3 Header	2	6-A	
3.3.1.4 Footer	2	6-A	
3.3.1.5 Cover page	2	6-A	
3.3.1.6 Watermark	2	6-A	
3.3.1.7 Equations	2	6-A	
3.4 Create and manipulate page backgrounds.			
3.4.1 Format a document's background	1	7-A	
3.4.2 Set a colored background	1	7-A	7-1
3.4.3 Add a watermark	1	7-B	7-2
3.4.4 Set page borders	1	7-A	7-1
3.5 Create and modify headers and footers.			
3.5.1 Insert page numbers	1	7-C	7-3
3.5.2 Format page numbers	1	7-C	7-4
3.5.3 Insert the current date and time	1	7-C	7-3
3.5.4 Insert a built-in header or footer	1	7-C	
3.5.5 Add content to a header or footer			
3.5.5.1 Custom dialog box	1	7-C	
3.5.5.2 Manual entry	1	7-C	7-3
3.5.6 Delete a header or footer	1	7-C	
3.5.7 Change margins	1	8-A	8-2

Objective Domain	Level	Topic	Activity
3.5.8 Apply a different first page attribute	1	7-C	
4.1 Insert and format pictures in a document.			
4.1.1 Add captions	3	4–C	4-3
	2	2-D	
4.1.2 Apply artistic effects	2	4-B	4–2
4.1.3 Apply picture styles	2	4-B	
4.1.4 Compress pictures	2	4-B	4-2
4.1.5 Modify a shape	2	5-B	5-3
4.1.6 Adjust position and size	2	4-C	4-3
4.1.7 Insert screenshots	2	4-D	4-4
4.2 Insert and format shapes, WordArt, and SmartArt.			
4.2.1 Add text to a shape	2	5-B	5-3
4.2.2 Modify text on a shape	2	5-D	5-5
4.2.3 Add captions	3	4-C	4-3
	2	2-D	
4.2.4 Set shape styles			
4.2.4.1 Border	2	5-B	
4.2.4.2 Text	2	5-C	5-4
4.2.5 Adjust position and size	2	5-D	
4.3 Insert and format Clip Art.			
4.3.1 Organize ClipArt	1	4-A	
4.3.2 Add captions	3	4-C	4-3
	2	2-D	
4.3.3 Apply artistic effects	2	4-B	4-2
4.3.4 Compress pictures	2	4-B	4-2
4.3.5 Adjust position and size	2	4-A	
4.4 Apply and manipulate text boxes.			
4.4.1 Format text boxes	2	5-A	5-1
4.4.2 Save a selection to the text box gallery	2	5-A	
4.4.3 Apply text box styles	2	5-A	5-1
4.4.4 Change Text direction	2	2-B	2-2
4.4.5 Apply shadow effects	2	5-A	5-1
4.4.6 Apply 3-D effects	2	5-A	
5.1 Validate content by using spelling and grammar checking options.			
5.1.1 Set grammar	1	6-A	
5.1.2 Set style options	1	6-A	
5.2 Configure AutoCorrect settings.			
5.2.1 Add or remove exceptions	1	6-A	

Objective Domain	Level	Topic	Activity
5.2.2 Turn on and off AutoCorrect	1	6-A	
5.3 Insert and modify comments in a document			
5.3.1 Insert a comment	3	2-C	2-3
5.3.2 Edit a comment	3	2-C	2-4
5.3.3 Delete a comment	3	2-C	2-4
5.3.4 View a comment			
5.3.4.1 View comments from another user	3	2-F	2-7
5.3.4.2 View comments inline	3	2-F	
5.3.4.3 View comments as balloons	3	2-F	
6.1 Apply a hyperlink.			
6.1.1 Apply a hyperlink to text or graphic	3	4-D	4-4
6.1.2 Use a hyperlink as a bookmark	3	4-D	
6.1.3 Link a hyperlink to an E-mail address	3	4-D	
6.2 Create endnotes and footnotes in a document.			
6.2.1 Demonstrate difference between Endnotes and Footnotes	3	4-B	
6.2.2 Manage footnote and endnote locations	3	4-B	4-2
6.2.3 Configure footnote and endnote format	3	4-B	
6.2.4 Presentation	3	4-B	
6.2.5 Change footnote and endnote numbering	3	4-B	4-2
6.3 Create a Table of Contents in a document			
6.3.1 Use default formats	3	5-E	
6.3.2 Set levels	3	5-E	5-7
6.3.3 Set alignment	3	5-E	
6.3.4 Set tab leader	3	5-E	
6.3.5 Modify styles	3	5-E	5-7
6.3.6 Update a table of contents			
6.3.6.1 Page numbers	3	5-E	
6.3.6.2 Entire table	3	5-E	
7.1 Set up mail merge.			
7.1.1 Perform a mail merge using the Mail Merge Wizard	2	9-A	9-1
7.1.2 Perform a mail merge manually	2	9-A	
7.1.3 Use Auto Check for Errors	2	9-A	9-1
7.2 Execute mail merge.			
7.2.1 Preview and print a mail merge operation	2	9-A	9-1

D | Microsoft Office Word Expert 2010 Exam 77–887

Selected Element K courseware addresses Microsoft Office Specialist (MOS) certification skills for Microsoft Office 2010. The following tables indicate where Word Expert 2010 skills are covered. For example, 3-A indicates the lesson and topic number applicable to that skill, and 3-1 indicates the lesson and activity number.

Objective Domain	Level	Topic	Activity
1.1 Configure Word options.			
1.1 1 Change default program options	1	1-B	1-2
1.1.2 Change spelling options	1	6-A	6-2
1.1.3 Change grammar checking options	1	6-A	
1.2 Apply protection to a document.			
1.2.1 Restrict editing	3	6-F	6-6
1.2.2 Apply controls or restrictions to document access	3	6-E, 6-F	6-5, 6-6
1.3 Apply a template to a document.			
1.3.1 Modify an existing template	2	8-A	8-1
1.3.2 Create a new template	2	8-B	8-2
1.3.3 Apply a template to an existing document	2	8-A	8-1
1.3.4 Manage templates by using the Organizer	2	10-A	
2.1 Apply advanced font and paragraph attributes.			
2.1.1 Use character attributes	1	3-A	3-1
2.1.2 Use character-specific styles	1	3-E	3-6
2.2 Create tables and charts.			
2.2.1 Insert tables by using Microsoft Excel data in tables	1	5-A	
2.2.2 Apply formulas or calculations on a table	2	2-C	2-3
2.2.3 Modify chart data	2	2-D	
2.2.4 Save a chart as a template	2	2-D	
2.2.5 Modify chart layout	2	2-D	2-4
2.3 Construct reusable content in a document.			

Objective Domain	Level	Topic	Activity
2.3.1 Create customized building blocks	2	6-B	6-2
2.3.2 Save a selection as a quick part	2	6-B	6-2
2.3.3 Save quick parts after a document is saved	2	6-B	6-2
2.3.4 Insert text as a quick part	2	6-A	
2.3.5 Add content to a header or footer	2	6-A	
2.4 Link sections			
2.4.1 Link text boxes	2	7-D	7-4
2.4.2 Break links between text boxes	2	7-D	
2.4.3 Link different sections	2	7-B	
3.1 Review, compare, and combine documents.			
3.1.1 Apply tracking	3	2-C	2-3
3.1.2 Merge different versions of a document	3	3-C	3-3
3.1.3 Track changes in a combined document	3	2-E	2-6
3.1.4 Review comments in a combined document	3	2-F	2-7
3.2 Create a reference page.			
3.2.1 Add citations	3	4-F	4-6
3.2.2 Manage sources	3	4-F	4-7
3.2.3 Compile a bibliography	3	4-F	4-6
3.2.4 Apply cross references	3	4-E	4-5
3.3 Create a Table of Authorities in a document.			
3.3.1 Apply default formats	3	5-D	
3.3.2 Adjust alignment	3	5-D	
3.3.3 Apply a tab leader	3	5-D	
3.3.4 Modify styles	3	5-D	5-6
3.3.5 Mark citations	3	5-D	5-5
3.3.6 Use passim (short form)	3	5-D	
3.4 Create an index in a document.			
3.4.1 Specify index type	3	5-B	
3.4.2 Specify columns	3	5-B	
3.4.3 Specify language	3	5-B	
3.4.4 Modify an index	3	5-B	
3.4.5 Mark index entries	3	5-B	5-2
4.1 Execute Mail Merge.			
4.1.1 Merge rules	2	9-A	
4.1.2 Send personalized email messages to multiple recipients	2	9-A	9-1
4.2 Create a Mail Merge by using other data sources.			

Objective Domain	Level	Topic	Activity
4.2.1 Use Microsoft Outlook tables as data source for a mail merge operation	2	9-A	
4.2.2 Use Access tables as data source for a mail merge operation	2	9-A	
4.2.3 Use Excel tables as data source for a mail merge operation	2	9-A	9-2
4.2.4 Use Word tables as data source for a mail merge operation	2	9-C	9-5
4.3 Create labels and forms.			
4.3.1 Prepare data	2	9-C	9-4
4.3.2 Create mailing labels	2	9-B	9-2
4.3.3 Create envelope forms	2	9-B	9-2
4.3.4 Create label forms	2	9-B	9-2
5.1 Apply and manipulate macros.			
5.1.1 Record a macro	2	10-B	10-2
5.1.2 Run a macro	2	10-A	10-1
5.1.3 Apply macro security	2	10-A	10-1
5.2 Apply and manipulate macro options.			
5.2.1 Run macros when a document is opened	2	10-A	
5.2.2 Run macros when a button is clicked	2	10-A	
5.2.3 Assign a macro to a command button	2	10-B	
5.2.4 Create a custom macro button on the Quick Access Toolbar	2	10-B	
5.3 Create forms.			
5.3.1 Use the Controls group	3	7-A	7-1
5.3.2 Add Help content to form fields	3	7-B	7-2
5.3.3 Link a form to a database	3	7-A	
5.3.4 Lock a form	3	7-B	7-2
5.4 Manipulate forms.			
5.4 1 Unlock a form	3	7-B	7-2
5.4 2 Add fields to a form	3	7-A	7-1
5.4 3 Remove fields from a form	3	7-A	

Lesson Labs

Lesson labs are provided as an additional learning resource for this course. The labs may or may not be performed as part of the classroom activities. Your instructor will consider setup issues, classroom timing issues, and instructional needs to determine which labs are appropriate for you to perform, and at what point during the class. If you do not perform the labs in class, your instructor can tell you if you can perform them independently as self-study, and if there are any special setup requirements.

Lesson 1 Lab 1

Using Word with Other Programs

Activity Time: 15 minutes

Data Files:

C:\084584Data\Using Word 2010 with Other Programs\Employee Report.docx, C:\084584Data\ Using Word 2010 with Other Programs\Employee Changes.xlsx

Before You Begin

You will need to have Outlook 2010 configured to perform step 4 of this activity.

Scenario:

Your editor, Mary Coleman, asks you to update the Employee Report document with details from the Employee Changes worksheet. She would also like you to create a PowerPoint presentation from the report and email it to her for review at mcoleman@ourglobalcompany.com.

1. Open the Employee Report.docx file from the C:\084584Data\Using Word 2010 with Other Programs folder.

2. Insert a linked worksheet object for Employee Changes.xlsx.

3. Save the updated report document as *My Employee Report* and send it to PowerPoint, saving the new presentation as *My Employee Report Presentation*

4. Email the updated report to Mary Coleman.

5. Exit PowerPoint and Excel without saving the changes.

6. Save and close the My Employee Report document.

Lesson 2 Lab 1

Reviewing Documents

Activity Time: 15 minutes

Data Files:

C:\084584Data\Collaborating on Documents\Review Employee.docx, C:\084584Data\ Collaborating on Documents\Updated Mc.docx

Scenario:

You sent the employee report to Mary Coleman for review. She has reviewed and returned her marked-up copy. You now need to review the tracked changes and accept or reject them with appropriate comments before sending the document for her approval.

---

1. Open a blank document.

---

2. Merge the Updated Mc.docx file into the Review Employee.docx file.

---

3. Review the tracked changes, accepting and rejecting them, as needed.

---

4. Add comments explaining the reasoning behind accepting or rejecting the changes.

---

5. Save the document as *My Review Employee* and email it back to Mary Coleman.

Lesson 3 Lab 1

Combining Changes from Different Document Versions

Activity Time: 15 minutes

Data Files:

C:\084584Data\Managing Document Versions\Newsletter.docx, C:\084584Data\Managing Document Versions\Newsletter R1.docx, C:\084584Data\Managing Document Versions\ Newsletter R2.docx, C:\084584Data\Managing Document Versions\Newsletter R3.docx

Before You Begin

You will need a SharePoint server set up to complete this lab. You must be added to the SharePoint site and provided with full control permission. The Server command must be added to the Quick Access toolbar.

Scenario:

You had created a newsletter for OGC Properties, a real-estate brokerage firm, and uploaded it to the SharePoint server for review and approval. As you are relatively new to developing content for a newsletter, your document went through extra rounds of reviews. In the future, you hope to avoid these extra reviews by trying not to repeat some of the basic errors you had made while working on the newsletter. So, you decide to spend some time studying the edits from different reviewers. But you do not want to waste time checking out and checking in each version one after the other to view the changes.

---

1. From the **Shared Documents** page on the SharePoint server, navigate to the C:\ 084584Data\Managing Document Versions folder and upload the Newsletter.docx file.

---

2. Change the versioning settings to enable SharePoint create a major version of the document each time you check it in.

---

3. Check out the Newsletter document.

 Use the Newsletter R1.docx, Newsletter R2.docx, and Newsletter R3.docx files to create three new versions of the document with changes from three different reviewers. Finally, check out the document with the changes from the third reviewer, accept all the tracked changes, delete all comments, and then check in the document to another version.

---

4. Open the latest version of the newsletter document from the SharePoint server.

---

5. Open the first, second, third, and fourth versions of the document.

---

6. Combine the changes from the first and second versions in a new document.

---

7. Combine the new document with the changes in the third version.

8. Combine the new document with the changes in the fourth version.

9. Save the second combined document in a local folder on your machine.

10. Close all open documents.

Lesson 4 Lab 1
Adding Reference Marks and Notes

Activity Time: 15 minutes

Data Files:

C:\084584Data\Adding Reference Marks And Notes\Employee Reference.docx

Scenario:

You are in charge of tracking the performance of employees in your organization. Beginning with the second quarter, employee reports are to be saved at the end of every month in a single document so that the month-to-month results can be compared. To make it easier to find each month's information, you need to bookmark the monthly reports. You also need to add appropriate captions to the charts and tables so that they can be readily associated with their corresponding month. You now need to provide footnotes explaining variations in employee sales performance, and cross-references when referring to other monthly employee reports.

1. Open the Employee Reference.docx file from the 084584Data\Adding Reference Marks And Notes folder.

2. Bookmark the April Employee Report, May Employee Report, and June Employee Report headings.

3. Add figure captions to all charts, making sure that each caption contains the proper month of the particular report.

4. Insert table captions for all tables, making sure that each caption contains the proper month of the particular report.

5. Under the "Employee Performance" heading, insert footnotes at the end of each month's "Sales" text, doing your best to explain any monthly variations.

6. In May's employee report, insert cross-references to both the Services and Sales information with corresponding information in the April report.

7. Save the document as ***My Employee Reference*** and close it.

Lesson 5 Lab 1

Making Long Documents Easier to Use

Activity Time: 15 minutes

Data Files:

C:\084584Data\Simplifying the Use of Long Documents\Employee Report Master.docx, C:\084584Data\Simplifying the Use of Long Documents\Er Jan.docx, C:\084584Data\ Simplifying the Use of Long Documents\Er Feb.docx, C:\084584Data\Simplifying the Use of Long Documents\Er Mar.docx, C:\084584Data\Simplifying the Use of Long Documents\Er Apr.docx, C:\084584Data\Simplifying the Use of Long Documents\Er May.docx, C:\084584Data\Simplifying the Use of Long Documents\Er Jun.docx, C:\084584Data\ Simplifying the Use of Long Documents\Er Concordance.docx

Scenario:

The management feels that an annual employee report would be easy to refer to than the monthly report. You have been asked to include the January through June employee reports as subdocuments in the Employee Report Master document and to use the Er Concordance file to mark index entries. You then need to create an index, a list of figures, a list of tables, and a table of contents.

1. Open the Employee Report Master.docx file from the C:\084584Data\Simplifying the Use of Long Documents folder.

2. In the Employee Report Master document, below the "Tables" title, insert the Er [month] employee reports as subdocuments.

3. Insert a one-level table of contents.

4. Insert a table of figures.

5. Insert a table of tables.

6. AutoMark index entries using the Er Concordance file.

7. At the end of the master document, add a single column index with the page numbers right-aligned.

8. Save the document as *My Employee Report Master* and close it.

Lesson 6 Lab 1

Securing a Document

Activity Time: 15 minutes

Data Files:

C:\084584Data\Securing a Document\Annual Employee Report.docx

Scenario:

Even though it is only halfway through the year, you have been unexpectedly asked to provide the annual employee report. The report's properties need to be updated to reflect the new time frame. The report also contains your conclusions regarding salary increases. These conclusions aren't public knowledge and should remain somewhat private. Since there have been some questions as to who has access to the network location, you need to take measures to secure the document as best you can.

1. Open the Annual Employee Report.docx file from the C:\084584Data\Securing a Document folder.

2. In the Summary properties, update the title to read "Six-Month Employee Report."

3. Hide the "Six-Month Conclusions" text.

4. Update the entire table of contents and index to hide any references to the hidden text.

5. Protect the document so that it cannot be edited.

6. Password protect the document with a password of your choice and save it as *My Annual Employee Report*

7. Verify that the security settings work as specified.

Lesson 7 Lab 1

Creating a Form

Activity Time: 15 minutes

Data Files:

C:\084584Data\Creating Forms\Rental New Client Form.dotx

Scenario:

Your manager has asked you to finish the Rental New Client Form template by adding the Apartment Type and Rental Terms drop-down form fields, some Monthly Price Range check box form fields, and a Wants/Needs text form field to capture any specific client requirements. Your manager would also like you to add references in the letter to the new form fields to reduce unnecessary typing.

1. Open the Rental New Client Form.dotx file from the C:\084584Data\Creating Forms folder.

2. Unprotect the Rental New Client Form template with a password of ***p@ssw0rd***

3. Insert an Apartment Type drop-down form field with the following items:
   - Studio
   - 1-Bedroom
   - 2-Bedroom
   - 3-Bedroom
   - 4-Bedroom

4. Insert a Rental Terms drop-down form field with the following items:
   - Annual Renewal
   - Long-Term Lease
   - Month-to-Month
   - Rent-to-Own

5. Insert Monthly Price Range check box form fields for the following items:
   - <$500,
   - $500–$1,000
   - $1,000–$1,500
   - >$1,500

6. Insert a Wants/Needs text form field so that the client can enter their specific requirements.

7. Create bookmarks for the new form fields.

8. Insert cross-references to the bookmarked fields in the letter's first paragraph.

9. Password protect the form, test it, and save it as ***My Rental New Client Form***

Solutions

Activity 2-5

2. **True or False? The View Side by Side option allows you to tile horizontally all open windows.**

    ___ True

    _✓_ False

Glossary

bibliography
A list of references that is usually inserted at the end of a section or document.

bookmark
Markers within a document that enable users to quickly return to a given location.

CA
(Certification Authority) A third party certification authority that issues digital certificates.

caption
A phrase that describes an object such as a picture, graphic, equation, or table.

citation
A reference to any legal source of content.

coauthoring
A feature that enables you to work with others simultaneously on the same document.

concordance file
A document used to automatically mark index entries in another document.

cross-reference
Directs the reader to a particular location in a document.

data linking
The process of linking a textual or pictorial object to a data source.

digital certificate
An electronic file that contains unique information about a specific person.

digital signature
A content authentication tool that authenticates the sender of a file and ensures the integrity of digital documents.

endnote
A reference note inserted at the end of a document section.

footnote
A reference note inserted at the bottom of a page.

form field
A container inserted into a form that is used to collect a specific type of information.

form
A document used to collect information for a particular purpose in a consistent format.

hyperlink
A navigation tool that links the contents in a document to other specific content, thereby enabling you to directly navigate to the linked content.

IRM
(Information Rights Management) A service that permits users and administrators to define permissions to access presentations, documents, and workbooks.

Legal Blackline

Compares differences between two similar documents, displaying those differences in a new document.

master document

A document that contains links to other related documents called subdocuments.

Microsoft SharePoint Foundation 2010

A collaboration software from Microsoft that provides a central location for individuals working in a project team or functional group to share information and communicate with one another.

Microsoft® Office SharePoint® Server 2010

A collaboration and content management server that is integrated with the Office 2010 suite.

signature line

A line used to add a digital signature to a document.

Signatures task pane

A pane that lists all the signatures in a document.

source

Reference material from which content is borrowed.

subdocument

A document linked to a master document.

versioning

The process of recording and storing changes made to a document over the course of its development.

Windows Live SkyDrive

A service provided by Microsoft that allows users with a Windows Live ID to store and share files on the web.

Word Web App

The online version of the Word application that can be accessed by using a web browser.

Index

A
access levels, 161

B
bibliographies, 90
bookmarks, 64

C
captions, 75
Certification Authority, 151
citations, 90
coauthoring, 43, 45
collaboration stages, 18
comments, 26
concordance file, 104
cover pages
  inserting, 100
cross-references, 85

D
data linking, 2
  modifying, 2
  with an Excel worksheet, 2
digital certificates, 151
digital signatures, 151
document properties panel, 19
documents
  comparing, 58
  merging multiple versions, 60
  uploading to SharePoint, 53
  viewing version history, 55

E
endnotes, 69

F
footnotes, 69
form fields, 169
forms, 168
  protecting, 176

H
hiding text, 140
hyperlinks, 80

I
indexing, 103, 106
  subentries, 104
Information Rights Management, 160

L
Legal Blackline, 31

M
Mark Index Entry dialog box, 104
master documents
  subdocuments, 130
merge changes, 35
Microsoft SharePoint Foundation 2010, 43
Microsoft® Office SharePoint® Server 2010, 43

O
obsolete links, 3
outline
  heading styles, 6
  levels, 6
  Outlining tab, 7
  sending to PowerPoint, 8
  view, 6

Q

Quick Access toolbar
  sending an outline to PowerPoint, 8

S

setting passwords, 157
signature line, 152
Signatures task pane, 152
sources, 90

T

table of authorities, 117

  Use Passim option, 118
table of contents, 124
table of figures, 111
track changes, 24

V

versioning, 52

W

Windows Live SkyDrive, 44
Word Web App, 44